ECONOMIC CONSERVATIVE/ SOCIAL LIBERAL

Mark Bragg
Publisher, IndependentVoters.com

ISBN: 0615548946
ISBN-13: 9780615548944

TABLE OF CONTENTS

PREFACE

Try to imagine our country as a giant ocean liner. Try not to think of her as the *Titanic.* We are foundering in the storm of Depression (remember, economies don't get depressed; people get depressed). Every day, the various observers on deck (the media) keep us depressed by telling us how bad things are. No wonder we're depressed!

While we may weather the economic storm, we're going to have to do something about all that red goo that's been filling up our holds. It's ink. If we take on enough of it, our ship will sink, and we will all drown. Meanwhile, the crewmembers on the port side of our ship (that's the left or liberal side) keep calling us over to their lifeboats with offers of free food, free life vests, and free retirement. On the starboard side (that's the extreme right or really conservative side), the crewmembers are trying to charge us for access to the lifeboats. After all, it may be an emergency, but it's still a free market.

So here you and I are…milling about in the middle of the ship…attracted by the Left's search for fairness and equality but knowing that someone has to pay for everything. And we're already being overcharged just for the privilege of being on this ship. In *Economic Conservative/Social Liberal,* I offer many reasons why we, the Independent Voters, are the only ones who can possibly save our ship. If too many of us move to the left, we capsize. The same thing happens if we move too far to the right. Join me in the middle. There are many benefits, including the survival of our country. It's time to find things we can all agree on.

Mark Bragg
Publisher
IndependentVoters.com

INTRODUCTION

ECONOMIC CONSERVATIVE/ SOCIAL LIBERAL

I have been calling myself an economic conservative and social liberal for about fifteen years. Many other people are using these terms now, and I welcome you all to the fold. We are not a political party, but we are a political force. Most of us are actually independents because neither of the two existing political parties will have us—or better, we won't have them.

If you're an economic conservative, the Democrats think you love big business, worship excessive profits, and don't believe in global warming. If you're a social liberal, the Republicans think you hate all forms of business, think profit is a dirty word, and believe in global warming. In fact, most of us aren't extremists in either direction, but it would be comforting to have some definition…and some company.

As it happens, President Dwight Eisenhower was one of us. President Eisenhower announced during his first term, "When it comes down to dealing with the relationships between the human in this country and his Government, the people in this administration believe in being what I think we would normally call **liberal**; and when we deal with the economic affairs of this country, we believe in being **conservative**."[1*] That was during his first term in 1954. The definitions have changed, but the general orientation has not. After sixty years of social turbulence, we have entered into a period in which we may achieve total economic collapse. We must do something about that, or we will lose entirely our ability to provide for those who cannot provide for themselves.

Our challenge is figuring out how to unscramble the egg. Free market economics made us strong. Imposing socialism on the economic system has made us perilously weak. Although the liberals don't see it, their attacks on the economic system that has produced this extraordinary wealth have created an atmosphere of stagnation, and they have immobilized the entrepreneurs who could bring us out of it. Liberals criticize an economic system about which they know virtually nothing.

My father used to say "all generalizations are bad, including this one." In this series of essays, I generalize about principles with which most of us can agree as economic conservatives and social liberals. These broad statements are intended to trigger discussion, debate, and decisions among people who don't care much for the extremists of either political party.

The ineptitude of the George W. Bush administration made many independents jump the Republican ship in favor of a new direction. Plenty has been written about the political manipulation of our intelligence professionals that led us to launch the

1 * Presidential News Conference, January 27, 1954

war in Iraq. One insight left me particularly distressed. In the last year of his life, I spoke to retired Congressman Charlie Wilson, my next-door neighbor in Washington DC. Charlie knew a lot about war in the Middle East (as portrayed in the film Charlie Wilson's War). He was confident that President Bush II had invaded Iraq to finish the job he thought his father should have completed. That war may prove to be the most expensive mistake we have ever made. It cost us our fortune, destroyed our economy, divided our society, and killed thousands of our men and women and hundreds of thousands of Iraqis.

While 72 percent of Americans supported the war in Iraq at the outset, finding that we were there on a false premise has been pretty hard to stomach.[2*] Once 60 Minutes outed the lone Iraqi defector who lied about the weapons of mass destruction (WMD) premise, the whole engagement made many of us sick. The informant nicknamed "Curveball" lived up to his name. Few of us disagreed that Saddam should be deposed, but the absence of the much-touted WMD left us questioning our own support and the honesty of our leaders.

No one who was in leadership at the time has owned that mistake, especially not George Bush or Dick Cheney. But voters knew who should have owned it, and we made our position clear when we turned over both Houses of Congress to the Democrats in 2006. The Obama regime has now adopted the Nixon approach: declare the war over and leave the battlefield. That's OK with most of us, but it didn't happen nearly fast enough.

Conservatives would say it was Bill Clinton's inaction that brought on the September 11th bombings and the need to chase Al Qaeda in the first place. Clinton was too busy chasing skirts in the Oval Office to respond to the many opportunities to take out Osama bin Laden before 9/11 even when the White House national security team repeatedly advised him. However, it was appalling that the head of that team, Richard Clarke, waited until **after** 9/11 to hold a press conference touting his book bemoaning the fact that four presidents had ignored his warnings. If he had had any balls, he would have held that press conference before 3,000 Americans died.

The language of hope and change that permeated the Obama campaign brought many independents to the left side of the ship. But that hope quickly gave way to discomfort, fear, and even resentment from those of us who thought change would be good, even if we didn't know what he meant by that at the time. Now we know: Obama thinks he knows better than we do about running our lives and our economy. Although their interests are not well aligned, both small business and large ones know that Obama is wrong on almost every subject having to do with business matters. And we also know Obama thinks he is the Second Coming.

I hope we can reestablish consensus regarding some very basic principles. Free market economics is a good system if we stop the monster of dictatorial bureaucracy; personal liberty is worth fighting for, stupid political manipulation is not. Smart people who make smart decisions are not dependent on color, race, or much of anything but their intellect and character. It's good that we elected a black president, but just achieving that goal is not enough. It's important that any president knows what he or she is doing.

I have never cared that Barney Frank is gay. I really care that he didn't know a whit about finance and defended Freddie and Fannie as they lost billions and became insolvent. My dislike of his actions has nothing to do with his sexuality. It has everything to do with his competence. Barney is an economic liberal…meaning he knows virtually nothing about real-world economics. It's good he didn't run again.

We elect people to represent us. If we are ignorant, we can expect to have ignorant representatives. The socializing members of the unionized teaching profession have managed to eliminate both economics and civics from the high school curriculum all over America. Is it any wonder that our voters are ignorant about those subjects and many others? If you're reading this, you probably agree that liberals on the left and conservatives on the right have screwed things up almost to a point of FUBAR (f**ked up beyond all recognition).

If we, as independents, are going to save America, we had better hurry up. The politics of the extremes never stop. No matter when you read this, the political maneuvering is going on right now. If nothing else, we independents can force the extremists into rationality. If they don't get us on their side, they lose. And I, for one, won't support extremists in either camp. So let's get busy defining the middle. For now, we will call it "economic conservative/social liberal."

CHAPTER 1

ECONOMIC CONSERVATIVE/ SOCIAL LIBERAL

Some Basic Positions

The question might logically be asked, "What do elected or appointed government officials know about economics?" Better yet, what do they know about business? The answer is: very little. There are only a few people in senior positions in the entire Obama Administration with any business background at all. Virtually none of our masters in the bureaucracy have any successful business experience because they've spent their careers as bureaucrats or theoreticians.

It has become fashionable among liberals to attack business for its perceived unfairness. After all, someone is supposed to provide everyone with good jobs, aren't they? The jobs should come with health care and four weeks of vacation. We're all supposed to be equal under the Constitution and in the eyes of God, aren't we?

Although my father reminded me frequently that life is not fair, he kept trying to make it fair. He was a liberal.

The solution for liberals is to go into business for themselves and actually begin to employ people in wealth-producing jobs. In the meantime, nonplaying coaches and inexperienced critics have no place in the effort to expand our wealth and help people take better care of themselves.

Without free market economics, there are no resources to provide for the social services the liberals want. It is a strange irony that China has become more of a free market than we are. So in the interest of finding some kind of consensus to reclaim our economic liberty, here are some beginning thoughts.

ECONOMICS:

1. A free market economy in which people are free to make virtually all of their own choices has proven itself far better at enabling people to provide for themselves than socialism, communism, or other forms of collectivism have. Most of us support free enterprise because it works. People who say it doesn't work have never produced any wealth, run a business successfully, or accomplished much at all. After all, they're Economic Liberals. What can you expect? In Cuba, the state still controls almost everything. The military dictatorship keeps people poor by requiring that they work for "the people" instead of themselves, and wages remain near $20 per month. A free market economy would allow Cubans to create wealth and keep it for themselves, a powerful human motivator. After 60 years, it should be clear to everyone that Castro's dictatorship merely imposed poverty on everyone (except his cronies). No one should have to endure that kind of "equality."

2. There is now so much regulation in America that only big, rich companies can afford to comply with it all, making it that

much harder to start or sustain a new job-creating business. Regulation is the enemy of creative enterprise and certainly the enemy of small business. Some of it may be necessary, but not very much.

3. Big government has grown to regulate big business. Big business is the concentration of wealth and power. Overthrowing concentrations of wealth and power in favor of personal freedom and independence was and is the foundation of America. There may be good reason to break up the multinationals into smaller units owned by shareholders and employees. They may be able to hold the executives more accountable. We'll work on that when we take over.

4. Big, multinational companies don't give a crap about anything but profit. They aren't responsive to shareholders or workers. Their executives will do practically anything to grab more than their fair share, and they certainly don't give a goddamn about America. All the PR nonsense about how responsible they are is a lot of blather designed to shield the greedy executives from public complaints. Don't believe it. The whole system is set up to drive more money to people who already have lots of it. Concentrations of wealth and power are the enemies of free, democratic societies.

5. There is no way for American workers to maintain the "American way of life" while competing with the "Chinese way of life." Our minimum wage is $7.25, and there is no minimum wage in China. American executives took our technology, our capital, and our intellectual property and went overseas for only one reason: they can sell stuff back to America for the same price and make much bigger profits. When they make bigger profits, they get much richer. While that undermines our standard of living, we can use it against them. Keep in mind our trade deficit was $508 billion in 2014 alone. *3 At $30,000/

year (an average American job) that means we exported more than 17 MILLION American jobs in that one year. Over the last 25 years, those collective numbers are staggering.

6. We should tap that same greed that sent American jobs overseas in order to bring them back. Instead of asking the government to figure out how to balance our trade, we can *require* balance of multinational executives who want to sell us their stuff. Over the next five years, let's reduce the goods allowed into the country—first to $400 billion, then $300 billion the next year, and so on until there is balance. (Our trade deficit in 2014 was $508 billion.) If companies have to stop selling us their imported stuff, they will find ways to buy more or build plants in order to make stuff here. There would be no tariffs and no embargoes or saber rattling....just a requirement for balance. They will figure it out based on their greed and self-interest. The Smoot-Hawley Tariff was a government answer that failed. This is a free market answer that will work.

7. As mentioned earlier, the trade deficit is at $508 billion per year (2014). Much of that deficit came from *billions of dollars* in imported oil, a great deal of which came from nations that use the money to make war against us. We have *huge* domestic reserves of oil. If we want to keep commuting and driving to the grocery store, we must tap our own reserves. We should require responsibility from drillers but turn them loose to make us independent in terms of this resource. When OPEC, led by the Saudis, declared war on American oil production, our government literally had no response. We were rapidly approaching energy independence. If we were to stop oil imports from hostile nations and nations who sell us more than they buy (Saudi Arabia), we could achieve trade balance and energy independence very quickly.

8. Environmentalists had a good idea when they wanted to clean the air and water. But environmental extremists now control the U.S. government. They are stopping us from drilling, mining, grazing, growing trees for harvest, and even growing food! Environmental regulations are sending many companies and jobs out of the country. It's time for rational, productive people to take over and send the environmental crazies back to the commune. Their religious zealotry is helping to bankrupt us as a country. We cannot wait until we are starving to take control of the environmental movement. But maybe if you are hungry, you will be motivated to get off your ass and confront the environmental lunatics. There are a lot of them. They don't contribute much, but they have learned very well how to stop the rest of us from accomplishing anything.

9. We can't spend more than we take in anymore. The consequences of the stupid and extravagant spending of both political parties has to stop right now. Even Bill Clinton favored replacing welfare with work. With more than 50 percent of the American people getting some form of subsidy from government, we have created a welfare state like the world has never seen before. What part of *broke* don't they understand?

10. The government must stop subsidizing everyone. It's a con game, which has been a source of fleecing the taxpayers for decades. How much did you get from Uncle Sam for not planting cotton, Senator? Don't plant corn...we'll pay you. Plant corn. We'll pay extra for ethanol, even though it's a boondoggle—even Al Gore knows it was a boondoggle to pay out more than $7 billion in subsidies in 2010. 4* By 2015, taxpayers will have invested nearly $54 billion total to support production and use of corn ethanol. 5*

Stop paying all subsidies now! We don't have the money, and it screws up the free market. Subsidy reform and tax reform are urgently needed, but expect the lobbyists to howl.

SOCIALLY LIBERAL POSITIONS

1. Freedom *of* religion was a powerful impetus for the creation of America. Freedom *from* religion is implied and should be just as powerful. I really don't want you or anyone else imposing your religion on my government... not Islam or Christianity or any other creed. Our government will always reflect the predominant mores of the time, but they should remain a reflection and not an imposition from anyone.

2. The religious right believes that homosexuality is a choice. Gay folks have known for a long time that it is nature...it's God's way just as much as heterosexuality is. It's always been a bit of a wonder why the Christian right won't abide *that* part of God's will. And gay marriage has absolutely no impact on heterosexual marriage. Two people of like mind and inclination have a natural right to be together, and the state should not interfere. Religion has no business interfering in a loving relationship between two adults. When a couple enters into the secular contract of marriage, the church (any church) has nothing to do with it. It's also possible to have the marriage blessed by a minister in church, but it isn't necessary. This is the most basic element in the doctrine of separation of church and state.

3. Abortion is an inherently terrifying, painful, and emotional experience. Everyone, even caring men who have gone through it with their women, know its impact. The memory of the act stays with a woman for her lifetime. She never really forgets. But I do not choose to impose my religious

beliefs about abortion on anyone else. The woman, her doctor, and her Creator are the only committee that needs to make the decision. However, third trimester partial-birth abortion is hideous. The baby, who would likely survive otherwise, is "terminated." Almost everyone is opposed to third trimester abortions unless there is a legitimate threat to the mother's life.

4. Free, public education is a great American tradition. Lousy public education is destroying our kids and our country. Inner-city kids are also entitled to a decent, quality education without fear and intimidation. The whole education system should be privatized with rewards for success at both the student and teacher levels. The government/union monopoly on education has failed.

5. The federal government has made education almost impossible. The Department of Education has more than five thousand people making rules that teachers have to follow, and deciding how to spend $82.3 billion a year. 6* They don't issue guns to teachers to help them protect themselves from the goofballs they are forced to keep in their classrooms. We should abolish the DE and return authority to principals and teachers. They should follow antidiscrimination practices, but forcing kids to stay in bad schools with bad teachers is discriminatory on its own. The National Education Association has trivialized the teaching profession, making us believe that all teachers care about is money and retirement. Good teachers are better than that. There are plenty of good, nonunion teachers working in private schools for half the money and benefits of the NEA. It's way past time to give parents and students the freedom to go to good schools with good teachers… the ones they choose. It's also time to dissolve the NEA.

6. Social Security and Medicare are welfare programs. They were created to provide a retirement and health mechanism for people who couldn't provide for themselves, a noble cause that's been hijacked. These programs are now paying everybody whether they need it or not. I know five multimillionaire couples who are collecting tens of thousands of dollars each and every year. They will collect far more than they put into the system. And when the system runs out of money shortly, we won't be able to help anybody. We must raise the retirement age and the age for Medicare eligibility to seventy right now. We must stop paying this form of welfare to people who don't need it and who should be paying their own costs. We must also adopt a means test immediately for both Social Security and Medicare.

These are some positions intended to help you crystallize your own opinions, even if they're different than what's described here.

CHAPTER 2

CONSERVATIVE ECONOMICS

There is a huge difference between jobs that create wealth and jobs that consume wealth. The worst jobs consume wealth and stop the creation of wealth at the same time. Those jobs are known as "bureaucrats".

We have allowed government to seize control of something government knows nothing about: how to produce wealth. At the most fundamental level, government can create an atmosphere in which private enterprise can produce wealth. Or it can constrain wealth production as it has increasingly done for the last fifty years. Liberals don't know the difference between jobs that produce wealth (private enterprise) and jobs that consume wealth (government infrastructure projects) and jobs that constrain wealth production (regulators).

The rules and regulations come frequently in response to abuses of power. Careless manufacturing practices led to such high levels of toxic waste in Cleveland's Cuyahoga River that it caught fire. Something had to be done. Environmental regulations have come about because of abuses of responsibility primarily by big business.

Government consumes wealth by hiring people to enforce regulation. But it also has constrained wealth production in a way that makes us no longer the world's wealthiest nation. We are now the world's largest debtor, and most of us as independents aren't very happy about that. You've heard all the scary statistics. Our debt is increasing at the *"Average rate of* $5 billion per day"; if you include the obligations of the U.S. government that have no source of funding (known as "unfunded liabilities"), the national debt is only a fraction of what we really owe; more than half of the American people are now receiving some form of "income" from the federal government! The government had to take that away from someone else or borrow it.

Historically, Americans were proud that we took care of ourselves and shared with those who couldn't take care of themselves. Now, we are all trying to take more than we give, and it can't work. However, there is no such thing as "conservative economics." There is only economics, and it is neither conservative nor liberal. While the liberal "economists" like to sit on high and look down at the rest of us who are actually doing the work, not one of them has ever created a job that produced wealth. Their macro view (meaning the larger picture) is a reflection of productive people, not an analysis of how to accomplish anything.

Ronald Reagan frequently used the statement "It isn't that liberals don't know anything; it's that so much of what they 'know' just isn't so." That is especially true when discussing economics with liberals. New York Times columnist and Nobel Prize winner Paul Krugman is the current poster child for know-nothing economists. On a recent edition of an ABC News talking heads platform, Krugman insisted that the solution to weak job growth was the addition of more government stimulus, meaning printing or borrowing more money. If he says it over and over again, most liberals will believe he is right. He isn't. Government stimulus doesn't work. We have proven it decisively. After more than four trillion dollars of stimulus money, joblessness has actually increased. When the Federal Reserve has opted to print money that has no value behind it, it has caused no new jobs to be created. Instead, that huge amount of new, worthless cash has been spent by the wealthy customers of the money center banks to bid up the prices on the various stock markets. Those shares have no more value than before, only a higher price created by too much money.

You can see it for yourself if you understand a fundamental principle of economics: *government consumes wealth, it does not produce it.* Every time you hear someone say that increasing the federal budget creates jobs, you know you are listening to an ignoramus. The job that is created will add another bureaucrat who produces red tape, not wealth. Of course, some liberals believe that everyone should work for the federal government. During the depths of the 2008–9 Depression, Congresswoman Maxine Waters proclaimed that it was time to nationalize all the airlines. Thinking like that works well in keeping poor people poor.

But Congresswoman Waters addressed a big area for discussion without even knowing it, namely, the growing disparity between the rich and the poor. I'm very happy for Larry Ellison (chairman of Oracle) that he is personally now worth more than $49 billion. 7* Bill Gates, Warren Buffet, and all the billionaires have managed to gather a very large percentage of the fruit that has fallen from the free market tree. They have guards and dogs and moats to protect themselves. But it will never be enough when the system collapses and people in every income strata can't get food.

So we move on to the real economic subject of the day. How can we adjust the system to give everyone a chance to participate and a shot at succeeding? Bill, Warren, and Larry have signed on to a gift program to support a variety of charities. It would make more sense if they would fund more start-up businesses to create new entrepreneurs who actually produce exportable products and useful services. Recipients of charity may be grateful, but recipients of welfare payments feel very badly about themselves. Entrepreneurs feel very good, and are able to produce enough for themselves and some to give away. Perhaps you have all or part of a strategy for how to foster more start-ups.

We have a lot of smart people in America. Let's begin a real dialogue about how we adjust free market capitalism to create more people who support it. It's hard to be very enthusiastic about capitalism if you can't feed yourself. If the biggest beneficiaries of the capitalistic system don't recognize the declining support for that system and do something to adjust it, fewer and fewer people in this democratic society are going to be willing to defend them.

Should we limit the size of personal wealth? Should we force corporations of a certain size to use profits to buy out their shareholders in order to make their employees into owners? Should we tax passive investment profit at an even higher rate than we currently do or tax capital gains not at all? That might increase the rate at which profits are taken and reinvested by risk takers and entrepreneurs.

The rich get richer and the poor get poorer. That's true. Success breeds success. Also true. But ownership of 100 percent of the equity in American business is vested in less than 20 percent of the people. The top 1 percent have most of the control. What would conservatives do to try and improve equity ownership in America?

Many of them would do nothing, but that is no longer an option. Equity ownership produces a great deal of America's income. Liberals take as much as they can and give it away to people they believe don't get enough of the pie. We call it welfare:

food stamps, unemployment "benefits," Social Security, Medicare. And it all leads to dependency. The federal government has become the modern plantation owner. Unfortunately, most of the indentured servants will vote for Uncle Sam to continue owning them just because it provides security.

Instead of expanding the numbers of Uncle Sam's servants, let's find ways to free them from their addiction to handouts. Instead of the depression brought on by dependence, let's find ways to help welfare recipients find freedom and dignity. Liberals like the power of controlling people, and conservatives don't care much for welfare recipients. So here we are again: Independents will have to come up with the answer.

Liberals bemoan "income inequality." Conservatives think it's up to the individual to make his or her own equality. Both are extreme views. Hoarding of assets is causing increasing inequality. That approach to "democratic capitalism" can't survive much longer. It isn't communism, socialism or any other form of collectivism. But some bright people must figure out an equitable distribution mechanism soon. The people are getting restless. The era of "hope and change" is all but forgotten, and nothing has gotten better.

CHAPTER 3

ENTITLEMENTS R US

Getting Over the Entitlement Mentality

Some politician must have invented the word "entitlement." It means that "you deserve it," whatever *it* is. When a politician uses government "entitlement" money and "benefits" to get votes, he's really using taxpayer money to bribe voters. If you like to sit around doing nothing...if you like to take advantage of other peoples' money...if you like getting paid for not producing anything, then you love the "entitlement government." You are a welfare recipient by definition—someone who takes money from the government and gives nothing in return.

But if you have earned what you are getting, then you really are entitled to it. Whether it's your home that you paid for or your savings account or your hospitalization insurance, you're entitled to everything you've worked for. And in the philosophy that built America, almost nobody was ever entitled to anything from the government. Hardworking, productive people don't care much for the word, and they don't care much for the people who think they are entitled.

We Americans do believe in generosity. We are the first to step up to help those who *cannot* help themselves. But giving money to those who *will not* help themselves violates the American spirit of self-reliance. Most Americans will voluntarily share the shirts on their backs and the food in their kitchens. But if you try to take it away from them, you're eventually going to have a fight on your hands whether you're a robber at gunpoint or a federal bureaucrat.

So how have we become a nation dependent on a system that takes money from those who work for it and gives it away to those who simply want a free lunch? The answer is that we've accepted the idea we are all ***entitled***. The government has created programs like Social Security and Medicare with good intentions, but these programs promote dependency. It's even in the Constitution to "promote the general welfare." But, as it turns out, we are *all* part of the problem. If you have paid something into Social Security but you're able to take out much more than you paid in, you are the problem. If you paid a bit into Medicare but you're taking much more out of it, you are the problem.

These are government welfare programs, and if you are taking money from them, then you are a welfare recipient. If you have enough to take care of yourself without welfare payments, it's time for you to make the decision: do I take welfare from the government, or do I take care of myself with my own resources? If you are a self-respecting, self-reliant American, join with us in refusing to take out more than you have put in. Agree to refuse Social Security until you are no longer able to care for yourself. The same is true with Medicare. Help rebuild America. Stand tall. Be proud. Refuse welfare.

Join with us to help promote the independence and primacy of the individual. Here are our policy positions. First, Social Security was never intended for everyone. It was designed to provide for those who could not provide for themselves. It was originally called an "insurance program." It never was. It was a tax to provide welfare payments, but it was never called that because of the political inclination to spare citizens the truth. Over time, the "insurance program" became everyone's benefit program. The monies collected were supposed to be protected by the Social Security Trust Fund. Our "trust" was misplaced. Social Security funds are no longer sequestered. They have been used by presidents and Congress for many other purposes, and are now part of the General Fund of government operations.

In a politically motivated sleight of hand, everyone now gets to participate. But there isn't enough money left in the "savings account" of Social Security to pay everyone. Therefore, the involuntary "contributions" of today's young people are being used to support today's old people. It's the ultimate Ponzi scheme, but it was never planned that way. Unfortunately, the strongest political organization in America casts so much fear in the hearts of today's politicians that they can't even talk about Social Security reform, so the monster continues to grow. AARP represents thirty-seven million Social Security recipients who pay them sixteen dollars a year to protect their "rights," their entitlement to Social Security and Medicare. *8

There are many people taking Social Security who simply don't need it. Therefore, the first thing we must do is establish a means test for Social Security recipients. For example, it could say that if you have a net worth of *x*, you must sustain yourself until you have used it up. Then you can become a welfare recipient and take Social Security and Medicare. A neighbor recently described how he receives a million dollars a year from his business interests while he and his wife receive a combined forty-eight thousand dollars annually in Social Security payments. The entitlement mentality has reached absurd proportions.

It's the same with Medicare. Many seniors are taking Medicare money who could afford to provide for their own medical insurance. A means test must urgently be imposed. But, if politicians fear for their jobs, who will dare suggest such a radical transformation? Perhaps this action must come from the people who recognize the train wreck we have created.

In addition to a means test, we must immediately institute a cap on Social Security and Medicare benefits. No one should be able to take more out of the system than they have put into it, unless they have become otherwise destitute…part of a continuing means test. Because life expectancy is so much greater today than it was when the system was created, it is common for people to have put in a hundred thousand dollars in their working lives, only to take out three hundred thousand dollars in retirement. Therefore, an immediate increase in the retirement age from sixty-five to seventy is imperative, as previously mentioned.

The message is one of dire urgency. If we continue to fear the mere discussion of the problem, we will achieve no meaningful reform, and the monster of deficit spending will continue to grow until it devours us. We are already nearing the point where people and nations will no longer lend us the money to keep up the charade. When that happens, we will be unable to care for anyone.

As of mid-2015, the U.S. Government is spending $2 trillion annually on Medicare, Medicaid and Social Security. 9* That is more than two-thirds of all federal income. How long do you think this can continue?

CHAPTER 4

BOOMERS ARE REVOLTING

And I mean that in the nicest possible way. We were born into revolutionary times. World War II was over. Our parents had renewed hope. The optimism of postwar America led to a giant crop of children over the succeeding ten years. But the revolution had only just begun. We feared the mushroom cloud in our childhood. Our parents feared the Beatles. Many of us had to serve in Vietnam, and many of us protested the departure of our fellow generation's members for war. But you know all that.

You also know about the electronic revolution, the imported merchandise revolution, the explosion of housing prices, and the bursting bubble that resulted. But the scary revolution is just starting to be realized. While you weren't paying much attention, we managed to lose our work ethic. We began thinking more about consuming than about producing. In spite of our dislike for welfare recipients, we began to believe we were the "entitlement generation." It is that philosophical oxymoron that is bringing down our generation and our entire society. And that's revolting.

Barry Goldwater was viewed as the consummate conservative of his time. As the strongest advocate of free choice and individual liberty, he loathed welfare programs. He saw the emphasis shifting from working hard and producing goods and services to a culture that worshipped retirement, the ultimate welfare. From his book *Conscience of a Conservative* comes the quote:

"But there is also a positive evil in these programs: in effect, they reward people *for not producing*. For a nation that is expressing great concern over its "economic growth," I cannot conceive of a more absurd and self-defeating policy than one which subsidizes non-production."

Absurdity has increased dramatically since Goldwater's day. There are two extremes currently being scrutinized. In California, it is possible to serve as a public employee for thirty years and retire with 95 percent of your salary—most of that money coming from current taxpayers—for the rest of your life. Your surviving spouse will continue to get those benefits until he or she dies. You both will get free medical care. If you started work at twenty years of age, you can retire at fifty and collect for another thirty or forty years while doing nothing. The song was titled "Nice *Work* if You Can Get It" (emphasis mine). But too many people no longer seem to believe in the value of hard work. And many fifty-year-old "retirees" take other jobs while they're using up the public employees' retirement fund. Greece is a microcosm of California liberalism and, eventually, American liberal doctrine.

The second absurdity is found in the Social Security and Medicare entitlement programs. We have been forced to contribute to the Social Security system for more than eighty years. Originally, those contributions were placed into a "trust fund." It isn't clear who started doing so, but Lyndon Johnson was famous for having breached the Social Security Trust Fund to pay for the Vietnam War. The war was unpopular, and Congress was not inclined to increase taxes, so they simply stole our retirement funds and replaced them with more useless government paper, like IOUs. The idea that it's a "trust" is absurd. We simply can't *trust* Washington.

The system is destitute. You will see the apologists on the liberal side contend that it isn't broke even though the money has almost all been spent. They will say, "But the system is holding notes for that money from the U.S. government." This is an economically idiotic position. The U.S. government will have to borrow the money to pay off those notes, and soon no one will be willing to lend our government anything but a tin cup.

So if fifty-eight million of us are taking money from a system that doesn't have any funds, how soon will it collapse? 10* Hillary Clinton used to say that Social Security was all fixed during her husband's administration. That's bullroar. Nothing was fixed, and the hole is getting deeper by the hour—actually by the minute. But those of us now reaching the retirement age, baby boomers to be precise, are finally going to sink the ship of this country in a sea of red ink. The only salvation is that we all take a bucket in hand and start bailing the red ink.

We must demand that the retirement age be increased immediately, not at some time in the future. We have enjoyed the life-extending benefits of the dramatic, expanding reach of medical science. But we can't stop working and simply do nothing while others support us. The system won't survive if we continue to take that approach.

We must immediately institute a *means test* to ensure the system is supporting only those who cannot support themselves. Social

Security was never designed to support everyone, and there are many of us who simply don't need it. Those of us who can work must continue working and contributing. Otherwise, the ship will simply sink.

Finally, unless a retiree is *incapable* of being productive, we must stop the practice of letting people take more out of the system than they have put in. If one accepts the reality that Social Security and Medicare are welfare by definition, then there may be enough people who will refuse to take it on that principle alone.

CHAPTER 5

UNEMPLOYMENT "INSURANCE" HAS GONE BROKE

In 2011, the federal government notified California that it was sending more than $800 million to replenish the state's unemployment insurance fund. There was no indication of the source of the money. This is an interesting ploy: calling it "insurance" when the actual insurance pool ran out of funds a long time ago. Now, Uncle Sam continues borrowing money he doesn't have in order to pay folks to continue doing nothing. Like Social Security and Medicare, two programs that have been broke for a long time, unemployment benefits have now become a form of welfare also…a system that pays people for doing nothing.

We will never know how many of the eight million people now receiving this form of welfare would actually prefer to be working. 11* Another ten million have used up their "benefits" and are now apparently doing something to feed themselves, perhaps in the underground economy. In either case, we have witnessed the creation of a dependent class, people who *expect* to get money for doing nothing. And this doesn't even include all the forty-six million folks who are getting food stamps. 12*

The "something for nothing" mentality is more dangerous to us than all the Muslim extremists on the planet. And Economic Conservatives are worried about it. When you add to these numbers the fifty-eight million Americans who are taking Social Security, and the thirty-nine million Americans who are retired and are taking Medicare, the size of the "entitlement generation," both older and younger, becomes a frightening reality. 13* At the rate we are borrowing to support all these people, one can only guess what happens when no one is left to loan it to us and the payments stop. As of June,2015, our National Debt is approaching $20 Trillion 14*and the budget deficit (the amount we are borrowing this year) is almost $500 billion. 15*

Economic conservatives don't understand why liberals don't understand this. We continue to see programs, legislation, regulation, and rules making their way into the American economy without regard for their impact or their cost. How long can it continue? We may have to experience a complete meltdown resulting from federal insolvency to find out. The Federal Reserve's answer is simply to print more money (the insulting government newspeak phrase for it is "Quantitative Easing). Economic conservatives know this is foolish policy that will lead to the decline in the perception of the value of our currency and hyperinflation. We're doing it anyway.

So what can we do to stop the madness? Even positive thinkers are challenged. If we stop paying people who aren't working, what will they do? They can't go plant a garden. They don't have any land. And the feds are taking more and more land out of productive use. (They euphemistically call that "creating wilderness.") So how will even the formerly employed, formerly insured take care of themselves and their families? Here's a shocking answer: they're going to have to rely on friends and family; they're going to have to create work for themselves; they're going to have to borrow capital and open businesses that can support them. In short, most of us are going to have to figure out how to take care of ourselves.

It won't be easy. In 2009 and 2010, more than two hundred thousand new government employees were added to the country's payroll. They are working overtime to create new constraints on the creation of jobs. As the chairman of one Fortune 100 company said recently, it's much easier and cheaper to go overseas to create a new manufacturing plant. There are far fewer regulations. It's not that foreign workers aren't cheaper. They are. But the worst impediment to the creation of new jobs in America is the impact of federal, state and local rules and the lack of restraints on our trade deficit.

American capital is racing for the exits by going overseas to invest where lower costs and regulations are making it easier—usually much easier—to make a profit. There's that dirty word again. Liberals want to repeal the part of human nature that likes to make money, improve their lot, live better…unless poor people are involved. Then making more money is OK. So in an attempt to control human behavior, liberals make rules that stop people from doing just about anything productive. In the process, bureaucrats are doing many things that lower our standard of living.

The imposition of an ever-increasing minimum wage is an example. The federal minimum wage is $7.25 an hour as of January 1, 2012. The American economy has contracted by 26 percent in the last three years. Instead of increasing the minimum wage as some economists suggest, a reduction in the minimum wage would result in a great many more people being hired. However, accompanying such a reduction should be a sweeping reduction in the regulations that make it too expensive to hire new workers. That list will require another book.

Economic conservatives would also like to see a reversal of the expansion of the federal workforce. Instead of contracting like the private sector, Congress and the Obama administration have created a great many new federal jobs with their extraordinary benefits. It's very hard to get rid of a federal employee once hired. Such reductions in force would make sense to private sector workers who have been laid off, but instead, the federal workforce grows and grows on borrowed money.

Alternatively, the decline of the American economy should create a commensurate decline in the size and cost of the federal government. If the economy declines by 20 percent, federal workers should experience a 20 percent reduction in their pay and benefits. At least such a practice would lead federal workers to find ways to help the economy expand rather than driving it further and further into decline.

Part of the answer is a government *dedicated to the success of the private sector.* What a revolutionary thought! Is it possible to create an environment in government that makes government bureaucrats responsible for making policies that help in the creation of jobs and wealth rather than stopping it? The presidential candidate who promotes that idea is one we should all vote for.

CHAPTER 6

IMMIGRATION VIEWED AS AN INVASION

Conservative thinkers are ambivalent about immigrants. Most conservatives are the progeny of immigrants somewhere back in their lineage. Many immigrants are hardworking, loyal, and responsible. If they entered the country legally, they may actually be contributing to the general welfare. However, if they entered illegally just because they were starving to death, being persecuted in their homelands, or looking for a better life, conservatives tend to view them as invaders carrying pitchforks and shovels instead of rifles and grenades…even if they are contributing to the general welfare.

It is particularly upsetting to conservatives to find illegal aliens on the rolls of registered voters. Then we have illegal voters casting votes for candidates who reflect policies favorable to illegals. Generally, that means liberals. A significant majority of Latino voters cast their ballots for liberal candidates. They tend to align themselves with other people of color, notably blacks, and other disenfranchised social groups, such as gays. Together, blacks, Hispanics, and gays form a voting bloc generally supporting liberal policies and candidates. Conservatives have found few approaches to any of those voting groups because they think those groups are socially liberal. Occasionally, that position is not correct.

It was odd to discover, for example, that blacks and Latinos were the deciding factor in the California vote that made gay marriage illegal. But it was odd only until one realizes that many of the blacks voting in that election came from fundamentalist churches. Latinos, largely Catholic in their religious orientation, also voted heavily in favor of making gay marriage illegal. It is one of the few subjects where conservatives and a large number of liberals share a common opinion. But it isn't enough to bridge any gaps.

It is not clear what the liberal position is on illegal immigrants. One position is that, once here, they should be allowed to stay. It is also not clear if that position applies only to illegal Mexicans or illegal everybody since illegal Mexicans far outnumber illegal immigrants from any other countries. But every president since Ronald Reagan has found illegal immigration to be an intractable problem. Reagan even gave up on the idea of sending them all home in favor of an amnesty program leading to citizenship.

So the invasion continues. Most mean us no harm. Some, however, are criminals. Enormous numbers of illegals have made the health-care system approach the breaking point. If they are working illegally, they probably don't have employer-paid medical insurance. As a result of the federal "you have to take everybody" policy, emergency rooms have become the primary health-care source for most illegals. As long as we can borrow the money to support the Medicaid and other state health-care services for illegals, the rest of us won't complain too much. After all, they're fellow humans, and we are the most generous people on earth.

But time is running out. Increasing numbers of American citizens are being displaced in the health-care system because it is overloaded by illegals. The conservative approach is to seal our borders, continue returning captured illegals to their countries of origin, create manageable programs for temporary migrant workers (folks who do the agricultural jobs that "no one else will do"), and defund state and federal programs that provide free health care for illegals.

Liberals have proposed no solutions, just the new tax called "Obamacare" They seem to be satisfied with continuing to allow illegals to occupy the homeland at will, regardless of the economic impact on American citizens. However, benign neglect is not a policy. The absence of a policy is hurting our own people, and eventually, we are going to realize that. It could become a major area of disagreement within factions of the liberal power structure, but no one in that community has even begun to address the issue. It is time.

We are running out of resources. While it was a nice idea that we could be the social safety net for the world's displaced and downtrodden, it is clear we are no longer capable of providing that service. We are no longer the world's wealthiest nation; we are now the world's largest debtor nation, and it's getting worse by the minute. We must close our borders, regain our financial position of solvency, and then, we may be able to accept legal immigrants again without damaging our own citizens.

It is unclear why the feds have allowed so-called "sanctuary Cities" such as San Francisco. Is it possible that the rest of us can select which federal laws we want to obey? Neither the president, Gavin Newson, Jerry Brown or Kamala Harris (attorney general) expressed much concern about the death of Kate Steinle in San Francisco at the hands of an illegal alien. Therefore our national and some state policies favor foreign criminals that threaten our own citizens including legal immigrants. This is outrageous even to social liberals

In the interim, we must expand the Peace Corps and other social service programs in order to send liberals into those countries that need them to help build their economies and their societies in the liberal model. However, we may want to wait until we can educate the liberals in what works economically and what doesn't. We can start with our own American experience.

CHAPTER 7

ENTREPRENEURS AND BUREAUCRATS

By 2015, the stock market regained almost all that it had lost in the previous three years of depression, and had soared to new heights as the result of $4 trillion injected into the market by the federal reserve. That was the result of too many dollars chasing too few places to put them. The PR machine for both government and big business touted how the profitability of many public companies had increased, but they had no explanation for the concurrent expansion of the number of unemployed people. That is quite simple to understand: neither government bureaucrats nor news reporters have any experience with real job creation. They have never done it or they wouldn't be bureaucrats or reporters.

There is only one thing government can do to create an environment in which new jobs can be created: *Get the hell out of the way*! But, unless we have leaders with the support of the people to eliminate vast segments of the bureaucracy, that is simply not going to happen. Government thinks it is supposed to govern...namely, control the activities of the people. Nothing could be more devastating to free enterprise than for it not to be free.

Big business has regained and expanded profitability because of increased efficiency, that is by doing more with fewer people, mostly overseas. More than $2.3 trillion of their profits are being held overseas in countries where tax rates are significantly lower. In another clever example of government newspeak, they're calling this practice "Inversion." Wanting to keep their money from Uncle Sam's clutches actually serves to create job expansion overseas with companies that consider themselves citizens of the world rather than American companies with obligations to America. Globalization has brought us cheap products and very profitable public companies at enormous cost.

The practice of "inversion" shifts the cost of government back to the middle class and other American taxpayers. It forces the American government to borrow money to replace the taxes being withheld. Those same companies are eager to accept the protection of the U.S. Armed Forces, but they are unwilling to pay for it. It is arrogant and traitorous, but it's legal. Why?

Entrepreneurs, on the other hand, are the start-up guys—the people who create new businesses that create new jobs in private enterprise. The economic conservatives like to call that "creating wealth." Government jobs at best should create an atmosphere in which entrepreneurs can succeed, but that rarely happens. Instead, government creates more government jobs that consume wealth from people and, worse yet, those bureaucrats create red tape, regulations, and rules that stop the entrepreneurs from functioning successfully.

Entrepreneurs depend on capital sources. Capital sources, investors, primarily examine two things: risk and reward. How much risk investors are willing to take depends on how great they think the reward will be if the investment works out. Investors on Wall Street aren't creating jobs, they're merely betting on the profit-producing ability of the public companies in which they invest. Entrepreneurial investors are the ones with real balls. Half the time they know they will lose their entire investment...but the return on the successful investment makes it all worthwhile.

Unfortunately, we are mired in an era of frightened investors. Left-wing Nobel Prize-winning economist Paul Krugman continues to insist that there is not an adverse impact on the economy because of failing confidence in government. He refers to that view as believing in the "confidence fairy." He can say that because he has never created a job in his academically-insulated life. The current atmosphere, in which investors have no confidence, has been created by the Krugman followers, including Barack Obama, another famous figure with no experience in job creation.

Ask any entrepreneur. The reason they can't start new companies and create new jobs in the private sector is burgeoning lack of confidence in the American government, starting with its leader. There is an enormous amount of money sitting around on the sidelines, but *most investors are unwilling to risk it* regardless of the potential reward. Of course, the technology junkies are making IPO investments again, and some of the Silicon Valley venture capital firms will invest in technology start-ups. But it's a lousy time to be looking for capital for anything else.

Investors of every size are waiting for a change of attitude. What they really want is to see a government that is committed to the success of American businesses, not the one we currently have that is committed to controlling every move we make. Investors are unlikely to get what they are looking for, and, as a result, they are not very likely to re-enter the capital markets for entrepreneurs. Until we have a supportive government, there is little prospect of a resurgence of new business creation and the new jobs that come with it.

Imagine a government that is committed to your success. If you fail, it fails. That's not what's happening now. In a truly just world, we could hold bureaucrats personally responsible for undermining the rights of the individual. That's what the Constitution was written to protect: the rights of individual people. With a government dedicated to supporting and promoting success, perhaps even theoreticians like Paul Krugman might actually be able to start businesses and employ people. Until then, Dr. Krugman should keep his theories to himself.

CHAPTER 8

LIKE PRIESTS GIVING SEXUAL ADVICE

There are many things theoreticians can do; they can postulate on the way things ought to be; they can give advice on how things got to be; they can offer opinions on how a job should be done. But theoreticians don't know squat about how to actually *do* anything. It's one of the major reasons sports team owners don't like to hire nonplaying coaches, whose knowledge of a game is only theoretical because they have never played. It's like Catholic priests giving advice on sexual relations to married couples. They simply don't know anything about it.

So here comes the liberal team to take over control of American enterprise. Saying a *prayer* of hope is the *only* hope. The liberals have been following economic theoreticians for more than twenty-five years. When the Democratic National Committee, (DNC) chairman was Chuck Manatt, the Iowa farmer turned California lawyer and business banker, there were four years of hope that the Democratic Leadership Council might actually influence the antibusiness orientation of the previous fifty years. It did for four years until Manatt left.*

Instead of being pro-business, the Obama administration has been overrun with antibusiness people who continue to wonder why business is lousy. The answer is, of course, business is lousy because Obama and his people don't understand anything about running a successful business because none of them have ever done it. Moreover, their antipathy is so great that they won't even listen to business people who might be able to help them.

Most jobs are created on a small scale. Entrepreneurs are historically the engines that pull the job creation train. But entrepreneurs have been hamstrung by lack of capital availability, massive increases in regulation, and political leadership that doesn't know anything about starting or running a business. Unfortunately, the Republicans aren't much better. They talk a better game, but they have done little to create a pro-business environment because many of them are preoccupied with other topics.

It is long past time when politicians must turn to those who know how to create jobs—entrepreneurs. These are people who have an idea, create a business plan, raise capital from wherever they can find it, and stick their necks out as far as they can to create new businesses. New businesses create new jobs. Successful private businesses create new wealth. In contrast, the government creates jobs by taking wealth away from private business to pay people who consume wealth: bureaucrats, welfare recipients, foreign dictators, and so forth.

---

* While I was writing this book, my old friend, advisor and partner, Charles T. Manatt passed away. I have dedicated this book to him and my other deceased partner, Lyn Nofziger, long-time Reagan advisor who died in 2006. Both were truly great Americans.

If anyone ever bothered to consult the entrepreneurs who know how to create jobs, they would hear an earful. They would say regulations are expanding at an amazing rate. They are intended to promote the theoretical approach to achieving a desired outcome. Entrepreneurs know they more frequently achieve voluminous unintended consequences. For example, there are many social economists who believe an increase in the federal minimum wage will help the underemployed reach some kind of economic stability. The reverse would happen. Increasing the minimum wage would price many currently employed people right out of the job market.

Suggestions like that come from people completely without experience in job creation, as do most of the regulations being created currently. While most of us dislike the concentrations of wealth in the banking industry, the Dodd-Frank reregulation of the industry did little to help individual Americans. First of all, it was 2,200 pages long and was considered in Congress for precisely one week. Nobody read it. Your member of Congress had no idea what he or she was voting on. A similar thing happened with Obamacare. That act was 2,400 pages long and was only debated for thirty-six hours; even fewer members of Congress read that. Nancy Pelosi will live in history as the person who said "We have to pass it so we can see what's in it."

We are uncompetitive with a world that has far fewer rules and is attracting our job creators in droves. To address this, we should convene a working session of entrepreneurs, people who have actually created jobs, to review the impact of all federal and state rules and regulations on job creation. In such a meeting, there will be no theoreticians allowed. If you haven't created jobs, we don't care about your theories.

While we aimlessly debate a jobs policy and government stimuli, both of which will accomplish nothing, our people remain unemployed, our tax receipts are declining, and our dependency on an ineffective government is increasing. Our only hope is creating wealth through private effort. If we don't mobilize privately, the public mentality will succeed in maintaining our death spiral into insolvency and an inability to provide for anyone, even those who cannot take care of themselves.

CHAPTER 9

TRADE DEFICIT EQUALS JOBS DEFICIT

America buys much more from foreign countries than those countries buy from us. It used to be called the "balance of trade." That has really been a joke for a long time. There hasn't been anything but a deficit in our trade "balance" for more than thirty-five years. During that period, we have sent nearly $9 trillion more to our "trading partners" than they have spent with us. The worst of those years was 2006 when a consumption-crazy America spent $828 billion more on imports than we sold in exported goods and services. 16* Of the total deficit, nearly half was due to American imports of foreign oil. This gigantic gusher of red ink makes the Gulf oil spill look like a trickle.

In 2010 alone, the trade deficit was $635.3 billion. Divide that number by an average annual wage of $30,000 and you have 21 MILLION lost jobs! Ask the conventional free market economist, and he or she will tell you all the lost jobs in the current economy are just the way the free market cookie crumbles. Ask the twenty-one million unemployed Americans, and they'll tell you where you can shove that cookie. The truth is there is no such thing as an international free market. And the United States isn't very free either. There are government intrusions into every aspect of the American market for all kinds of reasons.

So let's just focus on our trade deficit for the moment. There are two major players in the trade deficit calamity that has befallen us: multinational corporations and radical environmental groups. While these two groups generally dislike each other, they are really working in unison to create massive domestic unemployment, the former group in manufactured goods and services and the latter in expanding our importation of foreign oil. Oil has been as much as half of our trade deficit.

Politicians, oil sheiks, economists and international executives all will claim that this is an intractable problem that doesn't lend itself to easy solutions. That's crap. Unemployed Americans agree that it's crap. They might say there is a simple solution: Shut the door and stop importing all that stuff we buy from people who don't buy from us! The economists would call that "protectionism" which, they say, resulted in the imposition of the Smoot-Hawley duty scheme that brought on the Depression.

So let's assume for the moment that the Constitution, which calls for the federal government to "provide for the common defense" actually means *economic defense* as well as defense from invading armies carrying rifles (or invading Mexicans carrying shovels). How might we demand that the feds protect us, economically? That's easy. Starting January 1, the American government announces its five-year plan to reduce our trade deficit by 25 percent each year until we regain balance, which would be done through reducing and then stopping imports when we reach that year's limit. Based on our 2010 deficit of $635 billion, we would stop incoming imports when their collective deficit value reached $480 billion. The second year, we would stop imports when their collective deficit reached $360 billion and so on until we reach zero.

In actual practice, the change would happen much more quickly. The same formerly American (now multinational) executives who got rich taking our capital and expertise overseas will now bring it back to America. In order to keep their foreign factories selling to us, they will figure out how to create American products to sell back to those same countries to achieve balance. The Office of the U.S. Trade Representative in Washington DC can take a long vacation. They've been impotent for long enough anyway and obviously have done little to protect the American people.

The imported oil situation is a bit more interesting. The wacko environmentalists have managed to stop American companies from reaching the vast American supplies of gas and oil. Therefore, we buy more than half our total consumption from the likes of Venezuela. Some would say the environmental extremists are sponsored by our enemies in order to keep the import oil dollars flowing outbound. While that may or may not be true, it would be more rational to keep importing oil if those who were selling it to us were required to buy just as much in our manufactured goods as we buy from them in oil. They would find things to buy very quickly.

The other possibility is that we free American oil producers—wildcatters and drillers—to go develop the enormous reserves on American soil. We actually have the world's largest oil and gas reserves, but we aren't allowed to get at them. Such a change in policy would require that the American people recognize the environmental extremists for the wackos they are and elect people who will revise the authority of the EPA, U.S. Fish and Wildlife Service, and the U.S. Army Corps of Engineers. Those agencies have been totally taken over by the environmental extremists, and they are enforcing rules and regulations without regard to their impact on humans. But that's a chapter all its own.

CHAPTER 10

I WILL TAKE CARE OF MYSELF

The theme is recurring, as Yogi Berra might say, all over again: "We want government to take care of us because we can't (or won't) take care of ourselves." Although this is the fundamental principle underlying all of the fighting for larger deficits and greater government spending, no one, especially politicians, seems to be willing to talk about it. They won't talk because of the sheer numbers of people who claim to be unable to care for themselves.

Every time Maxine Waters, the member of Congress from southwest Los Angeles, opens her mouth, it is to demand that the government do more than it is doing to provide for "her people," namely, inner-city blacks. The cost of welfare, payments from the government for doing nothing, was once blamed almost exclusively on African Americans, but that is no longer the case. During the deficit reduction and debt increase farce, AARP members, mostly white folks, were demanding that *their* welfare sources, Social Security and Medicare, be preserved "or else." The threat in many prime-time TV commercials was that this voting bloc of more than 50 million seniors would strike down anyone who dared threaten their welfare payments.

At the heart of the debate is the loss of our individual independence. If you are concerned about security, you may be prepared to give up some or all of your freedom to gain some form of security. It is a scale of extremes, but a scale you can use with accuracy. At the far left of the scale is absolute security, a state-controlled economy where you think you are secure and will be provided for until you die…a welfare state wherein there is no personal freedom. Greece is a current good example. At the right end of the scale is absolute freedom, but a complete absence of security. The state is dissolved to enable complete, unfettered freedom of thought and deed, probably a practical definition of anarchy.

Neither of the extreme conditions has ever lasted for very long. The complete security of the communist system crumbled from lack of production. They couldn't coerce people to produce for the common good. Secretly, everyone was out for personal gain, but anyone caught at personal enrichment was shot so that the communist bosses could take the product of the offender and enjoy it themselves. Anarchy doesn't last long either because, absent some organization and some framework of legality, not everyone will act honestly or responsibly. It turns out that most people actually want some form of representative government as long as it doesn't explode into the dictatorial bureaucratic monster that has become the American government.

The consequences of our overwhelming dependency on government should be obvious to any rational person. Unfortunately, while there are many rational people in our society, many of us do not use our thinking mechanism very often or very well when it comes to government activities. Frequently we don't know what government is doing on our behalf. And, frequently, government also doesn't know what it is doing on our behalf. The process of creating a dependent society is insidious. Barry Goldwater used to liken the process to boiling a frog. Start out with cold water, and by the time the frog realizes he's cooking, it's too late to jump out.

Greek society was the foundation of Western Civilization. Today, Greek society is the model of welfare state deterioration. Gradually, the Greek people wanted to be paid more and more for doing less and less. Eventually, they wanted to be paid more still for doing *nothing*. As they produced less and less, the government had to borrow more and more to support the increasingly idle citizenry, and if the politicians refused, the citizenry would vote them out. Sound familiar? It's happened in America, and there may now be too many dependents to reverse the process. The AARP will vote out those who threaten their welfare payments. When our savings and borrowing are totally exhausted, they will regret their threats.

At one time, Americans were defiantly independent. We disdained welfare recipients as a dependent class unable to take care of themselves. But now that we have figured out that the enemy is *us*, we are in desperate need of a philosophical makeover. Welfare recipients often hate themselves because humans don't like to be dependent on others. Apologists on the left complain about lack of self-esteem among minority populations when they promote the very programs that create dependency and destroy self-esteem! When we were strong, independent individuals, we were a strong, independent country. Re-establishing that independence and individual responsibility will lead us back to the country we (and the World) admired.

The first step is to refuse the government heroin of welfare programs of every kind, including Social Security and Medicare, except for the people who are simply incapable of supporting themselves. The Greeks waited too long. Americans shouldn't.

CHAPTER 11

LIBERALS AREN'T STUPID. HOWEVER...

It is becoming a little difficult to understand how the left side of the political aisle believes we can forever continue to borrow as we have been. Is it a total disregard of reality or a belief in the debt fairy? Do we ever stop borrowing? Will the people who have the money (China, George Soros, Warren Buffett) keep loaning it to us no matter how deeply in debt we continue to slide? Or do they believe that we will somehow earn our way out of it even though our people continue to be idle and our multinational corporations continue to create jobs elsewhere?

Certainly it is necessary that the people who enjoy our national defense, our banking insurance system, our interstate highway system, and the various other valuable functions of the federal government should actually help pay for those services. The Republican "no tax" folks aren't really arguing for no more taxes on the rich. They seem to be saying we won't allow more taxes on the rich until you stop flushing that tax money down a rat hole. The legitimate costs of government seem to have been overwhelmed by expenditures that don't make sense…except possibly to the people who are taking the money.

Using the Paul Ryan (R-WI) statement that 70 percent of the American people now receive some form of payment from the federal government, it would appear that 30 percent of us are now supporting the other 70 percent. 17* Those of us in the working class can only produce so much, leading the feds to borrow the difference. But really, do the liberals believe we can keep doing this forever? They aren't stupid…or are they?

China has withdrawn from the U.S. bond market. Without their demand for bonds, we can assume the prices for treasuries will fall as the demand falls, but that will result in a rising interest rate to attract other buyers. That's just normal supply and demand. But what makes liberals think the U.S. government is any more or less susceptible to the pressures of rational financial management than the average American family? If a family spends too much on its credit cards, if it borrows too much against its house, or if it uses up all of its cash on things that don't bring in revenue, aren't they going to go broke? Many financial experts say America has already reached the point of no return. We just aren't psychologically prepared to admit it.

The liberals must stop spending. The conservatives must raise taxes. We must put our financial house in order. Most Americans agree with that premise, but our collective leadership is apparently incapable of getting the message. It needs to be delivered more strongly, and soon. This has been the focus of the Tea Party message, which has given the liberals cause to demonize the Tea Party. But what's wrong with the message, "Live within your means"? For economic conservatives, it is hard not to agree with the Tea Party's premise.

Stock analyst Jim Rogers told CNBC that America is already bankrupt, saying the United States keeps up the charade of rolling our debt over and over again. But he suggests America will never pay her debts. Standard & Poors rating service suggested a similar conclusion when it downgraded America's credit rating. A credit rating for America has the same meaning as credit ratings for individuals: how likely you are to repay your debts. Without a major change in our spending habits, the answer is: "not very likely."

But don't try to have that conversation with a liberal. Perhaps they inherited their money and believe it will always keep coming. Perhaps they are recipients of government funds and believe they will always keep coming. In both cases, such beliefs really come from believing in the existence of a debt fairy.

CHAPTER 12

YOUR ABORTION IS NOT MY PROBLEM

Men are pigs. It is in our genetic make-up to behave as pigs, especially when we are under the influence of too much testosterone and in the presence of women. Sex makes us particularly pig-like. It is important for women to remember this when you are being seduced. Men will say anything and do anything to get to your sensitive, delicate, caring, loving womanhood. I am a man, and, therefore, also a pig. However, I am sounding the alarm: our responsibility for our actions dissolves completely in the heat of passion. Remember that.

It's fun to watch Rachel Maddow on MSNBC. She's obviously very, very bright. Just ask her. She is also at least as condescending as Bill Maher, but without the slightly redeeming humor. And she is as predictable as the sunrise. Witness the interview with the very nice, well-meaning, and very upper-middle class lady from NARAL, the National Abortion Rights Action League. They weren't really talking about abortion rights, but rather who was going to pay for the abortions the league is promoting.

In their view, these poor, uninsured or underinsured, young, disadvantaged, and needy women have figured out how to get pregnant and want someone else to pay for getting them unpregnant. Free condoms weren't enough, because you actually have to go to Planned Parenthood to get them, and, in the heat of passion, that's just too much bother.

Unprotected sex gives these women several opportunities. First and foremost is the opportunity to become pregnant against their will, or at least against their preference. Second is the opportunity to become infected with some other unwanted, but equally preventable condition. Last is the opportunity to get someone else to pay for the treatment of both conditions. Are you sympathetic yet?

Abortion, as the Supreme Court has suggested many times, is "settled law." And, although it isn't settled in the minds of religious fundamentalists, Catholics, and other religious antiabortion advocates, the really unsettled aspect is the enormous cost imposed on society in serving the vast majority of these careless women. Victims of incest, rape, and other sexual crimes deserve our help. Victims of carelessness do not. And the co-perpetrators of this carelessness, the men, should be held equally accountable.

The sexual revolution of the last forty years has thrown off the yoke of four thousand years of misinformation, suspicion, and ignorance. Unfortunately, it has created a new era of misinformation, suspicion, and ignorance. Looming large at the front of the list of ignorant assumptions is the expectation that nonparticipants have some responsibility for paying for remediating the consequences of irresponsible intercourse. Instead of requiring the unsatisfied taxpayer to fork over the funds for abortion, aftercare, and grief counselling, let's total the tab and present it to the careless couple. We can give them a payment plan, but let's make them pay for their own actions.

In this new approach, before she is provided with abortion services, the pregnant person must identify her partner. Together, they must make arrangements for a payment plan to reimburse the generous taxpayers who have fronted the cost. It should bear interest at the cost of funds to the government. Such a plan will achieve dramatic results. Assuming the program is enforced by private collection agencies, there will be far fewer abortions. The word will get around: Don't get laid if the taxpayers aren't getting paid.

Greater use of condoms will be another result of this new plan for payment, ensuring far fewer cases of sexually transmitted diseases (STDs). Fewer infectious diseases mean a greatly reduced burden on medical care facilities for the indigent. Requiring personal responsibility for the sexual aftermath will cause a revolution in awareness of many other areas of personal responsibility. "Be prepared to pay for your own actions" might eliminate the entire deficit.

Abortion has always been a personal choice. The wealthy could go to foreign countries, and the poor went to back alleys or unlicensed practitioners. Prohibitions against abortion have always originated in religious doctrine the believers imposed on the nonbelievers. Religious passions against sex frequently trumped lustful passions. But the NARAL advocacy is no longer about abortion. It's about who will pay for it. The social liberal believes in abortion rights. The economic conservative believes in the taxpayer's right not to pay for someone else's mistakes.

I'm not quite sure what Fox News believes on this subject. They do tend toward the religion-based positions of the conservatives, including the former Governor and Reverend Mike Huckabee, a decent guitarist. In the likelihood that Roe V. Wade is going to stand for awhile, perhaps even he would endorse a plan that reduced abortions and disease using this carrot and stick (or condom and invoice) approach. It's better than coat hangers in a back alley.

CHAPTER 13

MODERN METAPHORS: KIM AS ROLE MODEL?

I seem to be spending more and more of my time trying to get away from the Kardashians. They're everywhere. The problem I am having is trying to figure out *why* they are everywhere. They don't *do* anything. They haven't really accomplished anything other than managing to be everywhere. They're just like Paris Hilton: famous for being famous. There is a huge portion of our society that has become vapid and vacuous. The Kardashians also happen to be voluptuous, but they are still vapid and vacuous.

I chose to lead with my analysis of the Kardashians because they represent the dichotomy of American society in the twenty-first century. Kim became internationally famous for her sex-tape appearance with a notorious black guy with a large endowment. He was some famous actor or rapper or something. She was the equally well-endowed daughter of a famous lawyer and stepdaughter of an indolent, former American hero, Bruce Jenner. Her beautiful face is enhanced for some (not me) by an ass that inspired the saying in the black community, "Why don't you back that thing up"?

Conservatives should love this family as well. No one in American history has been able to make a giant business generating giant profits by promoting themselves for no apparent talent like Kim Kardashian. She sure didn't look like she was acting in the video. I don't know how much she made from the sale of that video, but it must have been substantial. So this girl really does have a passion (pardon the phrase) for making money. What could be more conservative?

And we are learning far more about the family than we should. Long sessions with a shrink, fights with boyfriends and husbands, weeping over the loss of an earring; the participation of every family member and the ubiquitous nature of their activities ensure we may never get away from the Kardashians. Unfortunately, they are becoming the symbol of America to the rest of the world. Just like half of America, they don't actually do anything productive. They represent the rich and idle part of American society the rest of the world has come to resent.

If one combines the Kardashians with the Jersey Shore characters and the Real Housewives from wherever, one has a real cross section of our society, and it isn't pretty. The cable channel that carries most of this stuff has found a niche in the cultural promotion world. Their programs aren't enlightening or educational, and their announcer is really annoying, but they are making money like nobody's business. Literally. And there's a good reason for it. Many Americans want to be like the Kardashians when they grow up: rich, idle, indolent, vapid, vacuous, and vacationing.

It's the curse of a formerly wealthy nation. When we were rich, we could afford to do many things for their cosmetic appeal—the "show value" that kept people quiet, but didn't really accomplish anything. We have been so entertained that we haven't noticed how much government is taking because it is done so easily through withholding and excise, all of which increases the cost of everything we buy. Poor people have no idea how much extra they are paying for food and everything they consume through hidden taxation. We noticed even less when the government was charging huge expenditures to our deficit credit card. Out of money? No problem. Just raise the credit limit.

Our excesses finally brought us to insolvency because we were spending so much money on subsidizing indolence and uselessness…similar to the Kardashian lifestyle on a grand scale. And instead of disdain for this kind of example, we seem to be lionizing it. The federal government emulates it, finding more ways of doing less at other peoples' expense. It always sounds good. Take care of old folks, even if they can take care of themselves. Impose new rules to control every possible human endeavor to make it cleaner, safer, fairer.

MSNBC has joined the bandwagon with their marketing phrase, "Move Forward," while Fox News spends a good bit of its airtime trying to move backward. But what are we moving toward? Economically, we are speeding toward the edge of the Grand Canyon while the Kardashians, the Housewives, and the Jersey Shore clowns play pinochle in the club car of the American train. As a nation, we are woefully uninformed about the speed and direction of our train, and the fact that our engineer has no idea what he's doing. Somebody needs to pull the emergency brake. And fast.

CHAPTER 14

GOD AND THE INDEPENDENT VOTER

The Reverend Jerry Falwell liked to assert the decisive role of evangelical Christians, the "Moral Majority," in the election of Ronald Reagan. Reverend Falwell, may he rest in peace, was frequently wrong, but he was never in doubt. Evangelicals certainly participated, but they were far from a decisive factor. Ronald Reagan won the presidency in 1980 because of who he was, not because of his exhortations for, or of, the Divine. One can find few instances of Reagan pandering to the religious convictions of his supporters, and he almost never made reference to his own, personal relationship to the Deity.

However, the Holy Rollers did succeed in infiltrating the Republican Party because of their organizational skills. Holding mandatory meetings every Sunday under penalty of hellfire and damnation motivates the "convinced." They became known as "the base." If candidates didn't cater to the base, they stood no chance of being chosen at the convention or in the primaries, let alone in heaven. Independents or "moderates" left the party in droves. The base, like most zealots, is a statistical minority committed to promoting their own principles, not a formula for attracting a majority at the polls.

This disproportionate influence of religious fundamentalists has had a devastating impact on the Republican Party's process. They may be able to choose the candidates, but they're having a tough time electing them to office. Economic conservatives have been largely displaced by the social conservatives. Texas Governor Rick Perry went so far as to sign a pledge against gay marriage. That certainly caters to the religious and social conservatives but blows away a great many independents who are economically conservative and socially liberal.

Moreover, this condition brings about frequent discussion of the undue influence of religion on politics. The evangelicals think there should be more. The liberals think there should be none. The rest of us are merely uncomfortable having someone else's idea of religion being imposed on us through government action. As mentioned earlier, freedom of religion implies freedom *from* religion, and many independents would like to keep their religious or spiritual independence.

God, him and herself, is actually the ultimate independent. The natural laws of the universe are neither conservative nor liberal. They're just laws. For example, it is natural law that you can't spend more than you take in. Deficit spending, therefore, is actually against the law. It is also natural law that you can't force other people to believe what you believe. In other words, you can't force your religion on anybody else. The targets of religious fundamentalism will probably reject you if you try to take away their freedom to choose.

So why would Rick Perry sign a petition to deny freedom of choice to gays? He may think gays are the creation of the devil, but independent voters are more likely to think gay people are simply another creation of God. There was too much religion in his campaign, so all of those Independents went elsewhere for their leadership.

How about Michelle Bachman? Her religious views were very prominent in her campaign. The same is true with Rick Santorum. Tim Pawlenty sprinkled a bit of religious salt and pepper on his political omelette, but not many diners showed up to eat it. And while there are plenty of religious folks in the Tea Party movement, they have not taken it over. Liberals are doing their best to characterize it as a religious movement to try and separate independents from the movement, but not many have taken that effort seriously.

The good news is that Rick Perry chose to show his evangelical stripes sooner rather than later. Prayer breakfasts, national prayer services, and religious condemnation of others aren't very political in the broadest sense, but it surely is defining. Better you should be able to scrutinize the devil you know rather than the devil whose secrets you don't know. However, in today's very secular society, religious zealotry is still a pretty sure way to win the Republican nomination battle, but lose the general election war. It is unlikely the Christian Right can give in to the temptation to organize for victory rather than falling on the sword of their principles before they ever get to go to war.

CHAPTER 15

WANT JOBS? WHO WOULD YOU ASK?

Let's say you're the president, and you want to create jobs for the unemployed. Who would you ask, bureaucrats or businesspeople? Now, don't think about this too long— seven years is too long. Decide right now. If you answered businesspeople, you would probably make a better president than the one we have right now. But after seven years of ignoring, criticizing, and punishing job creators and after creating an institutional disdain for the free market economy that made us rich, job creators are looking elsewhere.

American wealth is leaving America at an alarming rate in search of a friendlier environment. It is certain that the concentration of wealth in fewer and fewer people is one of society's biggest challenges. But chasing wealth away helps foreign countries and hurts American prospects. Worse yet, chasing the wealthy out hurts one group most of all. You guessed it: poor people. The rich have options. They can go where they are wanted. The poor have few options, and nobody wants them. Ironic, eh?

Liberals have long believed that there is only so much pie to go around, and they should be the ones to decide how the pie is divided. Economic conservatives believe that, in order to serve everyone, we should simply make more pie. Those without any pie tend to look to the socialists to provide them with pie. That philosophy simply guarantees that people who can't make pie will only get as much as they can beg from others. Eventually, when the pie makers grow weary of giving away pies, the beggars will starve to death because they just can't take care of themselves. We are running out of pie.

The super rich in American society feel so guilty about the amount of wealth they have been able to control that they have formed clubs to try and give it away. It's really annoying. Bill Gates, Warren Buffet (pronounced buff-ay), Larry Ellison, and other billionaires have formed an association of sorts to give large portions of their wealth to "charity." It's a nice palliative for their tortured, self-indulgent souls, but it is utterly self-defeating. When their money has been used up by people who cannot care for themselves, it's gone forever, requiring ever more charity.

Here's a better idea. These people with a lot of money could create a giant fund to provide capital to people who legitimately want to take care of themselves. Instead of giving them the "fish," or charity, teach them to fish for themselves and provide them with a boat and fishing tackle. Require them to demonstrate that they have taken fishing lessons. Require they invest all that they own alongside the capital-providers. If they lose, everyone loses. But it would be better than gifting capital to charity cases with no incentive to make it work in the short and long term. Better yet, when they are successful, the new fisherman can repay the investment to help others gain independence. What a country.

Certainly some of the investment would be lost in this attempt to help people gain independence. But gifting it away ensures that it's all used up with no prospect of creating independence. Of course, there are those who are simply incapable of caring for themselves, and charity is their only hope for survival. But there are far fewer of those than the media would have you believe. Almost everyone can do something! And, in doing something to provide for oneself, there is hope of personal dignity and long-term independence. In truth, very few people want to be welfare recipients.

Let's start a fund to help people who want to be independent and free. Freedom Fund is already taken. The name Teach People to Fish Fund might work. Get Bill and Warren and Larry and all the billionaires to put a few hundred million dollars of their chump change in the fund, and get experienced, retired businesspeople to help teach folks how to fish. Could it be any worse than what we have going on now?

CHAPTER 16

OTHER PEOPLES' MONEY

The stories are endless about the ability of the federal government to waste money. They have elevated waste, fraud, and abuse to an art form. And the numbers are so big most of us can't really comprehend them. For example, America flushed at least $110 billion down the drain in Afghanistan reconstruction. 18* One might ask what there was to reconstruct, but that would be less than generous. Estimates of fraud in the Medicare part of the welfare system range as high as 20 percent. 19* The late Wisconsin senator William Proxmire gave out the Golden Fleece Awards to federal agencies with the most grievous records of wasting taxpayer money. He stopped when the people who were wasting the money threatened to sue him.

The reason this foolish, often flagrant, practice continues is that no one is responsible or even pays much attention to the spending because it's other peoples' money! You are careful with your expenditures because it's your money. But who will you hold responsible for wasting your tax dollars on stupid projects? No one. Find a member of Congress willing to be held personally accountable, and I'll show you a person soon to be broke. Let's see if we can track down the chain of decision makers responsible for the reconstruction fiasco in Afghanistan. No chance.

It isn't that most of these people are thieves. Of course, some actually are stealing from you, and sometimes they get caught. Unfortunately, that doesn't happen very often, and theft is not nearly as obviously prevalent as stupidity. Repeated newspaper stories about rampant corruption in and out of the Afghan government didn't stop our federal employees from turning over billions of tax dollars to a government that refused to allow auditing of where that money was going...and it was our money!

There is a reason Hosni Mubarak was holding $30 billion in his bank accounts when he was deposed. America gave it to him! 20* Same with Gadhafi and who knows how many other recipients of American aid that was intended to assist malnourished and impoverished people but was redirected to the Swiss bank accounts of dictators and despots. Even with the most massive accounting operation in history, the Government Accountability Office and all the accountants in the federal government agencies that dole out your money can't put a stop to irresponsibility. Actual theft? Yes...when they can find it. But stupid misuse, not a chance.

The process is insidious. You elect someone to go to Washington to represent you. In a very short amount of time, lobbyists besiege your representative on behalf of people and organizations who have become dependent on federal money (your money). Everyone needs more of your money. The AARP needs more Social Security, the FAA needs more airport towers, FEMA needs more money to pay for disasters...and the process grinds on. You've heard the national debt is approaching fifty-five thousand dollars per person because we keep spending money we don't have. 21*It's way worse than that. The federal government has made promises for future payments that total five hundred thousand dollars per household, including yours. They euphemistically call it "unfunded liabilities." 22*

We are approaching the collapse of the ability of the federal government to provide its basic responsibilities because we have allowed it to squander so many of our resources. When those who have been careful with their wealth will no longer lend to a massively irresponsible government, that government will no longer be able to send out the welfare checks to over (one hundred-nine million people), which includes programs like: Unemployment, Temporary Assistance to Needy Families, (TANF), Medicaid, Supplemental Security Income (SSI), food stamps; Supplemental Nutrition Assistance Program (SNAP), Social Security and on and on. *23

The phenomenon of being irresponsible with other peoples' money isn't new or even American. It's ubiquitous throughout history. Give any set of bureaucrats and politicians an unlimited checkbook without oversight and, voila! Your money is gone, you're deep in debt, and there's no one around to accept responsibility. All will say, "It wasn't my fault."

So whose fault was it? It probably doesn't matter. We already learned that Lyndon Johnson raided the Social Security Trust Fund to pay for the Vietnam War. He got away with it, and Congress was complicit. Finally, Congress gave up the pretense and began treating Social Security as an item in the federal budget rather than an insurance program to support poor people when they got old. Then they decided that Social Security would be for everyone, regardless of need or cost or actuarial soundness. By then, Social Security funds had been used up, so the government needed to borrow from other funds in order to make Social Security payments. Your kids are already deeply in debt because of this.

CHAPTER 17

LEADERS VERSUS POLITICIANS

Real leaders rarely last very long. They usually become politicians. The American electorate has a hard time telling the difference. Leaders are those among us with the skills, intelligence, honesty, and integrity to do the right thing under any and all circumstances. Politicians are the elected people who do whatever it takes to stay in elected office because it's fun, it pays well, and there's no heavy lifting. They enjoy cocktail parties, adoring crowds, and wealthy constituents who need their help. They come up with banal ideas, legislation that few understand, and overpaid staff to protect their backs and their images. They especially like being important, and, without the titles, they wouldn't be.

So why is it that politicians are the best we've been able to find? You can find the answer in your own willingness to let strangers search through your underwear drawer. Nobody wants that, even if there's nothing remarkable in the drawer. And that's the level of scrutiny imposed on candidates for office. Whether it's the clowns from TMZ, the jesters from MSNBC or the attack dogs from Fox

News, even a candidate for dogcatcher has no personal life when reporters are around. And why do "journalists" do what they do? It's because mindless Americans watch the shows and buy the products of the sponsors of the shows. Is there any hope that will change? None whatsoever.

What we really need is a few good men and women with Lincoln's honesty, Ike's leadership skills, Truman's business experience, and Reagan's charisma. When we find such a person, you can be sure there will be plenty of paparazzi hovering near his or her garbage can looking for embarrassing trash. Therefore, we must add the quality of skin like a rhinoceros. Are you willing to step up yet?

Without you or others who meet the criteria, we are doomed. Politicians will continue to make decisions for us that are based on ignorance; we lemmings will continue to follow them into the sea, and only those of us who know how to swim without a government lifeboat will survive. The most troubling part of this equation is the almost endless schemes the politicians can devise to postpone the inevitable. The bailouts have not been solely of the industries that have been badly run, such as automobiles, banks, and home loans.

The shift to government support of everything that doesn't work on its own has created a dependency mentality that never asks the inevitable question: where will the money come from? There seems to be a presumption among politicians that there is no end to America's ability to borrow. President Obama promised a Billion Dollars in aid to Africa during his visit to Kenya in 2015. His only source of funds for that generous gesture will be more debt. Are you ready to pay for it?

Assume, for the moment, that these politicians are wrong. Assume there is a finite limit to our ability to borrow money we don't have to pay people to do nothing. Now imagine what happens when the money actually runs out. Will those who have become dependent on government largesse revolt, run wild in the streets, and demand food from those who have it? Will they Occupy Wall Street again and insist that all debt be cancelled and jobs be provided to all?

Knowledgeable leadership might be able to devise a plan to avert such a crisis, but he or she would have to survive a process that promotes maximum heat and minimum light. It isn't merely a competition of positive ideas between the Left and the Right. It is a circus of personal attacks of the media tigers against the hapless-clown-like candidates in the center ring. The professional politicians have their lion tamers; the audience (you) will enjoy the show as the clowns are eaten; nothing will change. Eventually the circus will go out of business. When the food is gone, the show will be over.

However, there is hope. If you are a successful businessperson, you know the trouble we are in, then you know how to help get us out of it. It will require some sacrifice—not like the Marines at Iwo Jima or the soldiers on Normandy's beaches. It's much less exciting to participate in your government, but it is just as important. In fact, without it, you can be certain politicians will continue to overwhelm leaders at every level until we end up with a dictator running an even more dictatorial government.

CHAPTER 18

NO RISK...NO REWARD...NO JOBS

Historically, small-business owners have been recognized as the creators of half the new jobs in the American economy. The other half has always come from the expansion of existing businesses, namely, the growth of public companies. Capital is the key, and the hierarchy is pretty simple and easy to understand. Investors look to the risk and reward prospects of a publicly traded stock because the company has been researched by experts; it has historical performance; and the company has prospects for future success. Small businesses, particularly start-ups, have a much more difficult path.

The first round of financing to start a new business is called the "friends and family phase." You go to your mom and dad, uncles, aunts, neighbors, and other friends to beg for money. It is a humbling experience. You have a great idea. It will make millions. No, you don't know anything about the market, but you know the idea will be a huge money-maker. And you know you can build this empire with just twenty-five thousand dollars (it will take at least $250,000), and you are absolutely certain the market is there, clamoring for this product (with absolutely no research to prove it).

This was the path of Bill Gates and Microsoft and practically every other business ever started in America. After friends and family come the angel investors, who often turn into the devil when things go really well or really badly. Then come the venture capitalists, frequently referred to as the vulture capitalists: a bunch of young business school technicians with an inflated view of their own capabilities and nothing but disdain for yours. Lastly are the public investors who buy your stock in an IPO (initial public offering). Nice going if you get there. You're a zillionaire. But you can't get there without getting through round one.

Today, round one is dead, period. There is a lot of money sitting around doing nothing. In fact, there is so much money that banks are paying nothing to attract money because they have more than they can lend. The federal regulators won't allow them to lend unless you, as an individual, can prove you don't need the money. That has always been the case with banks, but it is worse today than any time since the other Great Depression. Regulators are scared to death of risk. Forget the potential reward. They don't think that way, and that attitude has infected every money source in America.

The friends and family of society are scared to death. They are keeping their money like never before because of their fear of the future. If we finally get around to declaring that we are in the second "Great Depression," your friends and family don't want to risk investing their money when they should have saved it to buy food. That's why America is not producing new jobs. Our confidence in the future has been left in our past.

It doesn't help that our "American" public companies are holding back $2.3 trillion in profits overseas because they don't want to pay a 35 percent corporate tax on it. 24* They are negotiating for a one-time repatriation benefit of a 5 percent rate because they don't like the idea of flushing all that money down the federal rat hole of never-ending squander. But, in fairness to the useful parts of the federal government, our so-called American-based multinationals are not reluctant to take advantage of the "benefits" of American government. Those services do provide some international stability, patrol of the seas and the skies, building their roads and bridges, frisking little old ladies at airports, and all the other somewhat useful services.

Instead, our multinational companies are using their capital to create jobs overseas, and our friends and family are fearful of government bankruptcy and the oncoming larger depression. Instead of just a business plan for start-ups, we need a new business plan for America. The candidate who knows enough about business creation and management to make a compelling case for his or her business plan will win the next election. The plan will address the rewards of taking the risks to create new jobs. Eliminating the risk of government collapse will go a long way toward regaining our confidence in the future.

We could start by repealing the Eisenhower-era regulations that allow American companies to avoid paying taxes by keeping their profits overseas. It was a great idea at the time. Eisenhower thought that economic inequality around the world was the leading cause of war. He theorized that if we generous Americans took our know-how and our capital to developing countries to help them become wealthy, the likelihood of economic-based warfare would be reduced. The theory worked well beyond Ike's expectations.

However, there are now more than 72 formerly "American" companies who have abandoned America in favor of escape to other host countries. They've left because of greed. . . .keeping more money without regard for the impact on their homeland. They are traitors in a worldwide economic war on America.

Those companies and other "Multinationals" now have created economic monsters out of China, India, and almost every other "developing" country. Our tax-exempt companies make giant profits overseas and keep them there to avoid paying taxes. Instead of investing the profits in the United States, they use them to create even more enterprises that create jobs to sell more of their products to America. The generosity of the American people has created a system that is certain to eliminate every manufacturing job in America that pays more than twelve dollars a day. Please see the chapter entitled "Trade Deficit Equals Jobs Deficit" for some thoughts on an instant fix. Meanwhile, take a chance. Invest in an American start-up.

CHAPTER 19

ENVIRONMENTALISM—THE EXTREMISTS TOOK OVER

If you have no personal experience with environmental extremists, it's hard not to be supportive of the environmental movement. Who doesn't want clean air and clean water? But cleaning up the streams and the air was just the beginning of a movement that is now almost as big as the defense business. And it has become business by any definition. Let's start with payroll. There are literally thousands of so-called environmental organizations in the United States whose primary purpose is to perpetuate themselves. These organizations started out as advocates to save the trees or endangered animals or whatever, but they have become very big business.

You have probably never heard of the Equal Access to Justice Act. Congress passed this particularly stupid law in 1980 without much fanfare. It gives attorney's fees to private groups if they are successful when they sue the government. And many of them have become very successful. The Natural Resources Defense Council reportedly received $180 million from taxpayers (which we had to borrow from China) as the result of lawsuits against Uncle Sugar. The NRDC insisted that the U.S. Fish and Wildlife Service had to list a bunch of supposedly endangered species, and they settled their cases with their friends in the government so they could get paid off for suing the government. You, as a taxpayer, paid for it.

The Endangered Species Act (known as the "Endangered Feces Act" to one Ninth Circuit judge) is possibly the most abused piece of federal legislation since welfare was invented. This is welfare for biologists and attorneys, a sinecure for the irrational and the economically unproductive. Moreover, that law and all the other so-called "environmental protections" are being enforced by people who don't care if you are employed or fed or housed as long as they can impose their views on the rest of us. It's radical environmentalism with a particularly sinister objective: stop all human activities that utilize the earth's resources for human purposes.

The Constitution guarantees the government can't take away your property without "just compensation." What it does not say is that the government can't take away the use of your property for just about any reason they can conjure up. They can say your property is "wetlands" even though there is no water anywhere near your property. You have to prove you don't have wetlands, a very expensive and time-consuming ordeal for a small landowner.

They can accuse you of violating the Clean Water Act for bulldozing an open field 20 miles away from the nearest "navigable water" as they did with John Rapanos in Michigan. They wanted to put him in jail for ten years and fine him hundreds of thousands of dollars even though he did no damage in their jurisdiction. When the Supreme Court agreed with Rapanos, the Army

Corps of Engineers simply ignored the Supremes and changed their jurisdiction.

This is not about clean air or clean water. It is about brutal, dictatorial government bureaucrats who are creating serious injury to American citizens without oversight or consequences. They can get away with it under the rubric of "environmental protection" when it has nothing to do with anything but unchecked, dictatorial powers. Unfortunately, you may not become a victim of the environmental extremists if you don't own property. So maybe the story of how a thousand poor black people might have been saved from death during Hurricane Katrina will help you understand.

In his book, Green Gone Wild, Attorney and Constitutional Rights Defender David Stirling details the story of an attempt to place flood gates in the canal outside New Orleans to protect the city from just the kind of devastating flooding Katrina caused. Congress authorized the funds to install the massive gates, but the installation was stopped by an environmental group's lawsuit. Under the Endangered Species Act, the group claimed the seabed might be disturbed harming some shellfish if the gates were ever closed. The gates were never built and 1,200 people drowned. So what species is really endangered? 25*

There is a good chance you won't care about this issue because you either don't own land or you don't think you're affected. Most of the more egregious examples of regulatory overreach are found in the West, and the conventional press doesn't pay much attention to small farmers, ranchers and other landowners. But you will eventually become concerned when your food, energy and other resources are interrupted. For example, there are hundreds of farmers in the San Joaquin River Delta whose water supplies have been disrupted by the U.S. Fish & Wildlife Service because of a non-native fish that is not really in any danger.

Meanwhile, our food prices are climbing and our dependence on imported food is increasing.

It is not a radical response to want to preserve American abundance. So pay closer attention to what they're up to because what you don't know could starve you and your family.

CHAPTER 20

MY LIBERAL SOCIAL POSITIONS YOU CAN IGNORE

In this chapter, I've summarized my personal positions on several issues. In some cases, I've simply stated whether I believe that position matters socially. They are not "politically correct" on purpose. They are philosophical positions that, by definition, have no right answer. However, I do believe most of these positions are widely held.

1. **Abortion**—None of my business.

2. **My religion**—None of your business.

3. **Your religion**—Your business, but keep it out of my government.

4. **Immigration** – Seal the borders. Send back the criminals. Require employers to report all employee earnings. Charge

illegals for all public services they use. Do not pay them unemployment benefits, Social Security, and so forth unless they have paid into the system. And don't let them take out more than they put in. In fact, do that with everybody. Give them a chance to earn legal status, or figure out how to send them all home. Even Ronald Reagan couldn't figure that one out. What is the rationale for failing to enforce this law while enforcing so many others?

5. **Women's rights**—Women are equal, but they don't have to keep proving it. Women's Studies is a college major that doesn't lead to a well-paying job. Study "How to create a successful business" instead, and 'consider male and female job candidates based on their qualifications, not their gender.

6. **African Americans**—Our society will eventually stop noticing there are differences, but it has not yet. Doing so takes practice, and most white folks are new at it. Give us a little more time and experience. Every time I have an encounter with an individual black person, I marvel at how well I am treated. I hope it is because I treat black folks and everybody else the same way I want to be treated. It seems to me that's the formula for good relationships between people of different races, genders, sexual orientations, and food preferences.

7. **Affirmative Action**—This was the way liberal white people tried to make up for a history of bad treatment of black folks, ethnic minorities, various religious minorities and women. Unfortunately, it required discrimination in reverse against everybody else in order to give some balance and redress. Theoretically, it would have been nice if we could have said, "From this day forward, everybody has an equal chance to compete based on their character and competence." But there was simply too much bad history for that. The theory didn't work in practice, and just about everyone abandoned it. Black folks and other

minorities are still disproportionately poor, unemployed, and suffering. Maybe thoughtful people can get together and find a way to address inequality. I'll be at that meeting.

8. **Gay Marriage**—None of my business, either

9. **Gay Rights**—God, whoever you think he or she is, created them too. Being gay is a fact, and why would you care about it? You don't have to live as a gay person, unless you are one. Then, we should all leave you alone too. It's pretty clear that those of us who threaten, intimidate, or abuse gay people are really uncomfortable with our own sexuality. So get comfortable with yourself, and you won't need to hassle gay people.

10. **Environmental Extremism**—For my position on this, please see the chapter entitled "Environmentalism—The Extremists Took Over."

11. **Education**—Union bosses and bureaucrats control the system. They have created a toxic atmosphere for students and teachers alike. Private schools are just about the only places where students get a decent education, and they are too expensive for poor kids. Since everybody is paying for a system that doesn't work, maybe it's time to re-examine the system. Let's send our kids to magnet schools, charter schools, voucher schools—anything to overturn the mindset that money, benefits, and seniority are the only things that motivate good teachers. Good schools motivate good teachers, and good teachers motivate kids. The federal bureaucracy knows nothing about how to create either of them. But even the best teachers will tell you that the absence of parental involvement is the most difficult aspect of educating children. If you want to see improvement without your participation, you can expect to be waiting for a long time.

12. **Defense**—It is time for a much smarter approach to defense. We have proven beyond a doubt that we have the intelligence capabilities and the modern warfare technology to defend ourselves, but we continue to defend the rest of the world at our expense. If you include the retirement pay and health-care costs for our retired service members, our military budget is more than twice what all the other nations of the world spend *combined*! The subject is worth an entire volume, or maybe a library, of its own. But we must discuss this taboo subject. It's the next largest cause of our financial crisis, next to entitlement.

CHAPTER 21

MAKE MORE PIE?

Conservatives used to say that if you didn't like how the economic pie was being divided, you should make more pie. That was probably a good way to look at it when the ingredients for making pie weren't all in the kitchens of big business or big government. The power for having land or capital and making rules is now all beyond the control of the individuals who used to open the bakeshops of opportunity. Concentrations of wealth and power are beginning to look like the wealth distribution profile just prior to the French Revolution. You may recall that those who were encouraged to "eat cake" (a waste product) turned on their outnumbered masters in search of wealth redistribution.

Comedian John Stewart likes to refer to the ownership chart of the bottom half of American economic society, wherein 50 percent of the people own less than 2.5 percent of America's assets. Perhaps the creative and managerial class of rich folks is better educated, more motivated, and harder working than poor people, but justification for the increasing inequality between the haves and have-nots won't get much attention during the next revolution. The entrepreneurial class of job creators is vastly outnumbered by those demanding both jobs and welfare. There will be little opportunity for intellectual discussion while the job creators are being bludgeoned.

Until the whole society breaks down around the issues of wealth distribution, there should be some discussion about post revolutionary ownership issues. French Revolution leaders were somewhat egalitarian after their ascent to power, but Napoleon quickly whipped them into subservience to his power and ego. Hitler's rise came to a proud people looking for redemption after their humiliation in World War I. Americans don't know much about civil unrest except for the Watts riots, the Rodney King revolt, Ferguson, Missouri and a few other lesser incidents. So how will we react to food riots, general looting, and outright revolution emanating from college kids and Social Security grandparents when we no longer have the funds to feed them?

As a society, Americans don't believe these circumstances will ever be allowed to develop in our country. The fact that these conditions already have developed escapes those who are still able to buy four-dollar gallons of gas, five-dollar loaves of bread, and ten-dollar steaks. By the way, all of our food prices are up, and we are now importing 26 percent of our food. Forty-one percent of our entire corn crop is being used to produce ethanol, a fuel that corrodes engines and costs more energy to make than it produces. Worse yet, we spent more than $55 billion since 2004 to provide price supports to the corn farming industry, which is why there is very low unemployment in Iowa and Nebraska.

It's time for a series of Congressional-style hearings, but without the participation of Congress. Instead, Bill Gates, Warren Buffet, and Larry Ellison who are geniuses at creating wealth for themselves and a circle of other people, should lead the discussions. Mr. Gates has managed to convince the billionaire club to give away more of their wealth to charity. As mentioned earlier, the billionaires should consider creating a giant fund to provide start-up capital to creative, hardworking entrepreneurs who will create jobs, export products and services, and spread the wealth.

If our economic ship sinks, many of our fellow passengers will not survive. If you have no lifeboat or even a life vest, you will likely drown. So it is in everyone's interest that we come up with a plan most of us can agree on and begin to execute it immediately.

CHAPTER 22

AMERICA IS FUBAR. IT'S TIME TO START OVER.

Since social subjects have been largely ignored in this book, you can assume I consider your positions on social issues are very important, but only to you. America is broke, despairing and declining economically at a rate so fast it is almost unimaginable. It is time for Draconian measures that many people won't understand. The geniuses who have gotten us into this mess have been working overtime for so long, we may not be able to pull ourselves out of the nosedive, but we must try. Without Draconian measures, our fellow citizens will experience a depression far greater than the last Great Depression, and our pace in that direction is accelerating. It is less complicated than the genius governing class would have you believe. Besides, how have they been doing so far?

Here is a short list of emergency common-sense actions we desperately need in a society where sense is becoming less common.

1. **Entitlements**—Get used to the proposition that no one is entitled to anything. Because of untrustworthy politicians, bureaucrats, and academic eggheads, we are now in a fight for survival. Our military may be able to prevent an invasion by our enemies, but it's not ready to protect us from ourselves. For example, you may have been paying into the Social Security system, but the money has been taken and replaced with IOUs from Uncle Sam. When he can't borrow any more, your payments will stop.

   There are many people who are taking payments who are able to take care of themselves. If we keep paying them, then we can't pay you. As mentioned previously in this book, we need a means test right now, along with an increase in the retirement age, as our life expectancy goes up. Encourage AARP to get over it. Also, folks over a certain net worth need to pay for their own medical insurance and be dumped from Medicare. . . right now.

2. **Defense**—Our annual defense budget of $496 billion is more than all the rest of the world's defense budgets combined! Dwight Eisenhower warned us to beware of the military-industrial complex, but that was before lobbying became a business of $3.5 billion a year in Washington, all of it being paid to people who want to take more from government. We need to completely rethink our defense strategy, and we need to empower people inside the Department of Defense to do it. How would they do the job with half the money? While we supposedly aren't "at war," economic warfare is being waged against us by many of our so-called friends. That's a war that Congress can fight with Balanced Trade legislation.

3. **Trade Deficit**—Our 2014 trade deficit was $508 billion. That's better than our $700 billion deficit in 2006, but, at thirty thousand dollars per job, we exported more than seventeen

million jobs in 2014 alone. Our twenty five year total is more than $9 trillion more in goods that we purchased from other countries than they purchased from us. Understand where our unemployment is coming from? Government doesn't know how to fix that, but private enterprise does. Give the world five years to achieve balance with us by stopping imports from countries that don't buy from us to achieve balance. Make exceptions for the impoverished, but stop giving away our wealth before it's all gone. Start with severely reducing the amount we buy from our foreign oil suppliers. They are delighted American environmentalists are keeping us from developing our own enormous oil reserves, but they need to be buying more of our products.

4. **Environmental Extremism**—We used to be self-sufficient in food production with enough left over to feed the world. Environmental radicals inside the federal government are spending a fortune every year paying their friends in various groups to sue the federal government. It's lunacy hiding in sheep's clothing. Environmentalists have sent many jobs to other countries through the creation of regulations that accomplish nothing but the creation of jobs for bureaucrats. It's time to eliminate most of the regulatory schemes and most of the regulators who enforce them. Fix the Clean Water Act and the Clean Air Act and repeal the Endangered Species Act. If you're angry about exporting jobs now, just wait until you're unable to get food because of these wackos.

5. **Welfare Reform**—Bill Clinton got it mostly right. He required welfare recipients to actually do something for the money. Handouts create dependency. Dependency destroys self-respect. People who hate themselves do bad things. It's the absolute reverse of helping people. Welfare simply makes slaves who respond to the heroin of government handouts. Welfare makes liberals feel better because they don't know

how much damage they're doing to their victims. But when we run out of money to pay them, welfare recipients won't be able to take care of themselves, and they will revolt. Instead, let's create a system that requires effort in order to be given money. Eliminate the circumstances that make being a welfare recipient easy and convenient. Give money and food stamps to people who *can't* help themselves. Give nothing to people who *won't* help themselves or at least require them to *do something* in order to get paid; clean the parks and beaches, provide assistance to the elderly. . . anything but the mindless approach that encourages welfare recipients to have more babies so they can get more money from the government.

6. **Wealth Distribution**—Other than those who inherit their wealth, we assume most wealthy people are smart. The question is: are they smart enough to realize that it's time to tweak the system? And, if they are, how will the free market system be tweaked enough to give more people an opportunity to participate? It is safe to say that flushing money from rich people into the federal waste machine isn't the way. Instead of protests, we could use some thoughtful and creative effort from smart people on how to adjust things so more people can support the freedom to accumulate wealth. For example, if we passed a law prohibiting distribution of dividends until we had 95 percent employment, how fast would the rich folks figure out how to employ more of us? The secret is using the creativity, intelligence, and resources of people who know how to create wealth to figure out a system that lets more people in on the action. Without it, the concentration of wealth and power will continue until the next American Revolution. Then, Socialism will make everyone poor.

7. **Energy**—Conservatives complain that our failure to stop deficit spending now is merely kicking the can down the road. In

the same vein, waiting until oil runs out before developing alternatives is equally damaging. We cannot let the missteps or failures of the few companies like Solyndra cause us to return to the stone ages of scientific research, but that research should include economic feasibility. Solyndra produced a solar tube that couldn't get below three dollars a watt in cost of production while conventional solar panels are all over the place now for a dollar a watt. Let's exploit our conventional energy deposits while we develop alternatives as fast as we can, but not so fast that we raise our citizen's costs of power unnecessarily. A fifty-cent-per-gallon tax on gasoline would reduce its use, help reduce our trade deficit, and pay for infrastructure improvements like roads and bridges. Less driving will also help clear the air.

8. **Education**—It belongs in the hands of parents, teachers, students, and local administrators. You do not need Washington to tell you how to do it properly. Dissolve the Department of Education. Send the money we save as block grants to the states. Keep the rules in place that require fairness, equality of opportunity, and performance standards. Allow the states to use the funds to encourage outstanding performance in public and private schools. Let parents decide where their children should go, but before that can happen, parents need to get much more involved.

9. **The Federal Philosophy**—Government believes it has the right to govern. In America, that authority was supposed to come from the consent of the governed. Unfortunately, our so-called public servants have become our masters. Just try dealing with a federal agency. If you are treated with respect or processed efficiently, and if their demands are reasonable, you're in a foreign country. There may have been a time in our history when federal bureaucrats were interested in our success. If this was ever the case, no one alive now remem-

bers it. This is because federal employees know, as a practical matter, they can't be fired. They're going to get a paycheck whether you like it or not. Moreover, they're going to get a pension with medical benefits that are probably better than yours whether you like it or not.

Even the "good" federal employees know you can't touch them. Their superiority is generally worn on their sleeves. In the new era, federal employees will succeed only if the private sector succeeds. If we fail, they fail. When our paychecks dry up, so do theirs. If we lose our benefits and our pensions, so do they. If they become our supporters instead of our masters, we will enter Nirvana... heaven on Earth...so don't count on it. But it's nice to dream, isn't it?

10. **Your Involvement**—If you believe in the American Dream, you are not very happy about the nightmare in which we wallow. But, if you believe in it, you must get involved. City councils can't spend your money foolishly if you know about it. State representatives can operate in the darkness only if you leave your flashlight at home. Watch what they're doing. If you don't like it, work to throw them out. If you're honest; if you care about our country's future; if you have the guts to stand up to sensation-seeking reporters who know nothing about nothing—run for office. Don't give up. The hopes and dreams of our ancestors and our progeny depend on your participation.

"Surely evil will triumph if good men and women do nothing."—Virginia Bell Bragg (my Mom) - adapted from and with deference to Sir Edmund Burke.

Notes

[1] Presidential News Conference, January 27, 1954

[2] Ekins, Emily. "Poll: Americans Want Congress to Vote on Military Force Before Midterms, Say an Ebola Outbreak Is Likely and Kids Should Be Required to Get Vaccinations." Reason.com. Reason Foundation, 09 Oct. 2014. Web. 21 Aug. 2015. <http://reason.com/poll/2014/10/09/october-2014-reason-rupe-poll>.

[3] International Regional Science Review 29.3 (2006): 278-96. U.S. Census Bureau U.S. Bureau of Economic Analysis NEWS. U.S. Department of Commerce, 5 Aug. 2015. Web. 21 Aug. 2015. <http://www.census.gov/foreign-trade/Press-Release/current_press_release/ft900.pdf>.

[4] Wynn, Gerard. "U.S. Corn Ethanol "was Not a Good Policy"-Gore." U.S. Corn Ethanol Was Not a Good Policy-Gore | Energy & Oil | Reuters. Thomson Reuters, 22 Nov. 2010. Web. 21 Aug. 2015. <http://af.reuters.com/article/energyOilNews/idAFLDE6AL0YT20101122>.

[5] Cox, Craig, and Andrew Hug. "Driving Under the Influence: Huge Taxpayer Investment in Ethanol Yields Paltry Payoff." EWG. Environmental Working Group, 01 June 2010. Web. 21 Aug. 2015. <http://www.ewg.org/news/news-releases/2010/06/14/driving-under-influence-huge-taxpayer-investment-ethanol-yields-paltry>.

[6] Department of Education. "Education Department Budget by Major Program." Education Department Budget by Major Program 83.2143 (1936): 74-75. Education Department Budget by Major Program. U.S. Department of Education, 15 June 2015. Web.

21 Aug. 2015. <http://www2.ed.gov/about/overview/budget/history/edhistory.pdf>.

[7] Vinton, Kate. "The Richest Californians In Technology 2015." Forbes. Forbes Magazine, 5 Aug. 2015. Web. 21 Aug. 2015. <http://www.forbes.com/sites/katevinton/2015/08/05/the-richest-californians-in-technology-2015/>.

[8] AARP. "AARP's Mission, Vision, Advocacy, Community Service & Products." AARP. AARP, 01 Apr. 2015. Web. 21 Aug. 2015. <http://www.aarp.org/about-aarp/?intcmp=FTR-LINKS-WWA-ABOUT>.

[9] Centers for Medicare & Medicaid Services. "Vital Signs: Rise in National Health Expenditures Slows." National Health Expenditures 2013 Highlights 39.3 (2013): 1. National Health Expenditures 2013 Highlights. Centers for Medicare & Medicaid Services, 2015. Web. 21 Aug. 2015. <https://www.cms.gov/Research-Statistics-Data-and-Systems/Statistics-Trends-and-Reports/NationalHealthExpendData/Downloads/highlights.pdf>.

[10] U.S. Census Bureau, Shelley K. Irving, and Tracy A. Loveless. "Dynamics of Economic Well-Being: Participation in Government Programs, 2009–2012: Who Gets Assistance?" Dynamics of Economic Well-Being: Participation in Government Programs, 2009–2012: Who Gets Assistance? (2015): 1-29. Www.census.gov. U.S. Census Bureau, May 2015. Web. 21 Aug. 2015. <https://www.census.gov/content/dam/Census/library/publications/2015/demo/p70-141.pdf>.

[11] Bureau of Labor Statistics, and U.S. Department of Labor. "THE EMPLOYMENT SITUATION —JULY 2015." THE EMPLOYMENT SITUATION — JULY 2015 (2015): n. pag. THE EMPLOYMENT SITUATION — JULY 2015. U.S. Department of Labor, 7 Aug. 2015. Web. 21 Aug. 2015. <http://www.bls.gov/news.release/pdf/empsit.pdf>.

[12] FRAC, Food Research and Action Center. "Supplemental Nutrition Assistance Program Participation and Child Food Security." (2015): n. pag. Federal Food/ Nutrition Programs. Food Research & Action Center, 7 Aug. 2015. Web. 21 Aug. 2015. <http://frac.org/wp-content/uploads/2011/01/snapdata2015_may.pdf>.

[13] Social Security Administration. "Research, Statistics, & Policy Analysis-Monthly Statistical Snapshot, July 2015." Monthly Statistical Snapshot, July 2015. Social Security Administration, July 2015. Web. 21 Aug. 2015. <http://www.ssa.gov/policy/docs/quickfacts/stat_snapshot/>.

[14] U.S. Department of the Treasury Bureau of the Fiscal Service. "The Daily History of the Debt Results." Debt to the Penny (Daily History Search Application). U.S. Department of the Treasury Bureau of the Fiscal Service, 1 Apr. 2015. Web. 21 Aug. 2015. <http://www.treasurydirect.gov/NP/debt/search?startMonth=06&startDay=01&startYear=2015&endMonth=06&endDay=30&endYear=2015>.

[15] Congress Of The United States, and Congressional Budget Office. "An Update to the Budget and Economic Outlook: 2014 to 2024 ." An Update to the Budget and Economic Outlook: 2014 to 2024 (n.d.): n. pag. An Update to the Budget and Economic Outlook: 2014 to 2024 . Congressional Budget Office Nonpartisan Analysis for the U.S. Congress, 27 Aug. 2014. Web. 21 Aug. 2015. <https://www.cbo.gov/sites/default/files/113th-congress-2013-2014/reports/45653-OutlookUpdate_2014_Aug.pdf>.

[16] United States. Census Bureau, Foreign Trade. Foreign Trade. N.p., 5 Aug. 2015. Web. 21 Aug. 2015. <http://www.census.gov/foreign-trade/balance/c0004.html>.

[17] Umhoefer, Dave. "Has Ryan Remained Consistent in Talking about What He Calls Society's "takers" and "makers?"" Politifact Wisconsin. Tampa Bay Times, 13 Feb. 2013. Web. 21 Aug. 2015. <http://www.politifact.com/wisconsin/statements/2013/feb/13/paul-ryan/has-ryan-remained-consistent-talking-about-what-h-/>.

[18] Welna, David. "The Man Who Keeps Tabs On U.S. Money Spent In Afghanistan." NPR. NPR, 14 May 2015. Web. 20 Aug. 2015. <http://www.npr.org/sections/parallels/2015/05/14/406764884/the-man-who-keeps-tabs-on-u-s-money-spent-in-afghanistan>.

[19] Edwards, Chris, and Tad DeHaven. "Fraud and Abuse in Federal Programs." Downsizing the Federal Government. Cato Institute, Aug. 2009. Web. 21 Aug. 2015. <http://www.downsizinggovernment.org/fraud-and-abuse>.

[20] Ross, Brian. "Hosni Mubarak's Wealth: He's a Thief, But Not That Big a Thief." ABC News. ABC News Network, 11 Feb. 2011. Web. 20 Aug. 2015. <http://abcnews.go.com/Blotter/hosni-mubaraks-wealth-thief-big-thief/story?id=12897677>.

[21] Satista. "U.S. National Debt per Capita 1990-2014 | Statistic." Statista. Statista 2015, 2015. Web. 21 Aug. 2015. <http://www.statista.com/statistics/203064/national-debt-of-the-united-states-per-capita/>.

[22] Sherman, Amy. "Romney Says Debt plus Unfunded Liabilities Equals $520,000 per Household." Politifact Florida. Tampa Bay Times, 22 May 2012. Web. 21 Aug. 2015. <http://www.politifact.com/florida/statements/2012/may/22/mitt-romney/romney-says-debt-plus-unfunded-liabilities-equals-/>.

[23] United States of America. Bureau of Labor Statistics. U.S. Bureau of Labor Statistics. By Bureau of Labor Statistics. U.S. Bureau of

Labor Statistics, 12 Feb. 2015. Web. 22 Aug. 2015. <http://www.bls.gov/cps/cpsaat08.htm>.

[24] Rubin4, Richard. "U.S. Companies Are Stashing $2.1 Trillion Overseas to Avoid Taxes." Bloomberg.com. Bloomberg, 4 Mar. 2015. Web. 22 Aug. 2015. <http://www.bloomberg.com/news/articles/2015-03-04/u-s-companies-are-stashing-2-1-trillion-overseas-to-avoid-taxes>.

[25] Congleton, Roger D. "The Story of Katrina: New Orleans and the Political Economy of Catastrophe." Public Choice 127.1-2 (2006): 5-30